PRAISE FOR
OUR AMERICA

"Chekhov said that a work of art should 'melt the frozen rivers of the heart.' The text and the phenomenal photos of *OUR AMERICA* do just that. This book turns the ghetto into human faces. Its honesty, eloquence, and heart inspire action."

—Mary Pipher, author of *Reviving Ophelia*

"With an assist from the remarkable David Isay, LeAlan Jones and Lloyd Newman have become powerful story-tellers. Their tales, by turn, will charm and startle you. In a tour of their neighborhood and of their lives, these two young men remind us with a combination of fervor and grace that in America all is not right."

—Alex Kotlowitz, author of *There Are No Children Here*

"LeAlan Jones and Lloyd Newman have told us a story that should tear at our hearts. They speak of a 'different America.' One where crime, drugs, lack of jobs, and every imaginable social ill work to break the human spirit. Some youngsters rise above it, but too many of them don't have a chance. They are trapped. Read this moving chronicle and resolve to help a young person in need in your community to believe in the American dream."

—General Colin L. Powell

"You won't reach the last page of *OUR AMERICA* without wondering what country this book is about. The young authors, LeAlan Jones and Lloyd Newman, have given us dispatches from hell, bleak and numbing as anything from Vietnam. You despair of the waste of young lives but hope that at least two will be saved: the sensitive and perceptive young Jones and Newman. We rage and pray for them and their generation."

—Frank McCourt, Pulitzer Prize–winning author of *Angela's Ashes*

"This rough yet eloquent report from the edge of humanity forcefully reminds us that a new generation is even now struggling to survive on our urban battlefields, and to escape."

—*Kirkus Reviews*

"If all reporters had the hearts of LeAlan Jones and Lloyd Newman—and if all hearts were informed by the kind of reporting they do—then the world might at last become the kind of place these young men yearn for."

—Bob Green, columnist and author

"Through the voices of inner-city residents on Chicago's South Side, OUR AMERICA captures the devastating effects of high joblessness and segregated neighborhoods on individual family and social life. This is a moving and deeply disturbing book. If we are to have a more humane society, OUR AMERICA ought to be read by every policy maker and concerned citizen in America."

—William Julius Wilson, Malcolm Weiner Professor
of Social Policy at Harvard University,
and author of *When Work Disappears*

"Like flares sent up from within a besieged city, these children's voices call out to us. If the world of the black inner city exists for us chiefly through the imagination or the media, it is time we took a closer look, for the fabled mean streets are real. America will fall in love with these wisecracking boys as they try, innocently and bravely, to show and to explain the devastation that is all around them."

—Melissa Fay Greene, author of *Praying for Sheetrock*
and *The Temple Bombing*

"A frank and provocative view of America's minorities from the inside out and bottom up. . . . A powerful, rousing message for all concerned readers."

—Michael A. Lutes, *Library Journal*

Class picture of LeAlan and Lloyd in second grade.
LeAlan: sitting, second from right; Lloyd: first row standing,
second from left.

Life and Death on the
South Side of Chicago

OUR
AMERICA

LeAlan Jones and
Lloyd Newman

with
David Isay

Photographs by John Brooks

POCKET BOOKS
New York London Toronto Sydney

DEDICATED TO ALL PEOPLE
LIVING GHETTO LIVES

 POCKET BOOKS, a division of Simon & Schuster, Inc.
1230 Avenue of the Americas, New York, NY 10020

Text copyright © 1997 by LeAlan Jones, Lloyd Newman, and David Isay
Photographs copyright © 1997 by John Brooks
Photograph on p. 28 by Russ Berkman
Photograph on p. 154 courtesy of the Morse Family

Originally published in hardcover in 1997 by Scribner

ISBN-13: 978-0-671-00464-4
ISBN-10:   0-671-00464-6
First Pocket Books trade paperback printing October 2002

40 39 38 37 36 35 34 33 32

POCKET and colophon are registered trademarks of
Simon & Schuster, Inc.

For information regarding special discounts for bulk purchases,
please contact Simon & Schuster Special Sales at 1-800-456-6798 or
business@simonandschuster.com

Cover design by Matt Galemmo
Front cover photos: authors by John Brooks;
street scene by Arvind Garg/Gamma Liaison

Printed in the U.S.A.

Many times, many ways in America, young African-Americans do not get to speak their piece. In this book, you will hear about the lives of two African-American men growing up in the ghetto. We live in a second America where the laws of the land don't apply and the laws of the street do. You must learn our America as we must learn your America, so that maybe, someday, we can become one.

—LeAlan Jones

Do you remember when you walked among men?
Well, Jesus, you know as you're looking below that it's worse now than
    then.
They're pushing and shoving, they're crowding my mind.
Lord, for my sake teach me to take one day at a time.
One day at a time, sweet Jesus. That's all I'm asking of you.
Just give me the strength to do every day what I have to do.
Yesterday's gone, sweet Jesus, and tomorrow may never be mine.
Lord, help me today. Show me the way. One day at a time.

—Gospel Hymn

CONTENTS

CONTENTS

PREFACE

How rare it is to get behind the pervasive stereotypes of young black men and revel in their complex humanity! And how infrequent the chance to listen to the poignant and powerful voices of these fellow citizens. *Our America* provides this unique occasion. In a moment in this nation's history when we all make claims about the significance of our stories, those often overlooked are the most provocative and painful ones—the stories of America's teenagers in chocolate cities. The intelligence, courage, and hope in the stories of Lloyd Newman and LeAlan Jones are extraordinary and exemplary!

Two years ago, I was asked to the White House to discuss a possible speech by President Clinton on urban youth. In the meeting—attended by over twenty members of the President's staff and the cabinet—we talked about the immoral maldistribution of wealth, high levels of unemployment, dilapidated housing, decrepit schools, inadequate health care, unavailable child care, and shattered familial and communal bonds.

I then was asked, "Could you give us a list of the nation's top scholars and experts whom we should consult about these deplorable circumstances?" I replied, "It would be much better for President Clinton to sit and talk with ten young people from the 'hood for two hours—then he would have more than enough material for a serious and substantive speech." The conversation stopped. The room was silent. Then one brave staff person muttered, "The President lives a rather sheltered life and rarely has a chance to talk at length with young black teenagers." I paused, looked around, and said, "How many of you have sat and talked with young people of color from the 'hood for two hours?" Again silence engulfed the room. No hands. No replies. And I thought to myself: Is not democracy a process that highlights engaging, listening, and responding to the very people who are affected by the public policies enacted by the powerful? Would it not have been more difficult for President Clinton to sign a vicious and punitive welfare bill if he had sat and talked with the vulnerable children punished by it?

We shall never know. But with the appearance of *Our America*, President Clinton and the rest of us have a chance to listen and to learn—and realize that what is at stake is not only life and death in our cities but also the survival of our country.

—Dr. Cornel West

ACKNOWLEDGMENTS

Our America started out as two radio documentaries, *Ghetto Life 101* and *Remorse: The 14 Stories of Eric Morse*. For help on the radio pieces, much thanks to Earl B. King, president of No Dope Express Foundation, Alex Kotlowitz, Rick Madden and the CPB Radio Program Fund, Ann Blanton and the Chicago Community Trust, Ellen Baker, Shelle Davis, Linda Paul, WBEZ Chicago, Rick Karr, Sharon Green, Jude Doherty, Richard Nevins, Adrian Nicole LeBlanc, Gary Marx, Susan Orlean, Anna Vargas, Ellen Weiss, Pat Lute, Cindy Carpien, Bev Donofrio, Scott Lowell, Alex Chadwick, Donna Gallers, Bill Buzenberg, Delano Lewis, Dan Pinkwater, Sandy Tolan, Jay Allison, Ray Suarez, and Susan Stamberg. For music on *Remorse*, thanks to Reggie Marshall and the great Frank Morgan, who changed my life. Special thanks to Caryl Wheeler. Very special thanks to Gary Covino, who put more into both of these pieces than anyone could imagine.

For writing *Our America*, much gratitude to the Annie E. Casey Foundation for making the work possible. Also to Jody Buckley of America Online and Kathleen Jenkins and Torey Malatia of WBEZ. Thanks to Mary Rickard and Gallery 37 for helping us find John Brooks. Thanks also to Barbara Hall, Douglas W. Nelson, Joy T. Moore, Pastor Laura Robinson, Doug Burack and the accounting firm of Lutz & Carr, Suzanne Clores, Andrew Orlando, Lisa Lazarow and Friends Seminary, Elizabeth Crew and Charles Levy Transportation, Dr. Teddy Osantowski and Future Commons High School, Barbara

ACKNOWLEDGMENTS

Cavallo, Lois Abramchik, Henry Hassan, "Knowledge," Rhoda Murray, Kyra Payne, Marion E. Joplin, Donoghue Elementary School, Henry Cisneros, Phyllis Banks and the Chicago Housing Authority, Herschella Conyers, Michelle Kaplan, Rhoda Murray, all of the residents of Ida B. Wells—particularly those who live at 3833 South Langley, and the entire Morse family. Special thanks to Harvey Wang and Tom Maday for photography advice, and to our incomparable photo editor, Richard Sandler. Thanks to Michael Alcamo for legal counsel and his other vast and varied contributions to this project. Thanks to David Earle for transcriptions, and Stacy Abramson for transcriptions, advice on the manuscript, and tireless pursuit of foundation support. Very special thanks to my assistant, Melissa Stevens, who held it all together.

Thanks to our agent, Jonathan Dolger, for his wise and gentle handling of this project, and the enthusiastic and dedicated support of our editor at Scribner, Scott Moyers. Thanks also to Jennifer Chen, Nan Graham, Susan Moldow, and Pat Eisemann at Scribner, as well as Amy Einhorn and Nancy Miller at Washington Square Press.

Personal thanks to Dora Gomez, my friend Dan Collison, my partner Erica Meinhardt, and my family—especially my mother Jane, who, as always, was my chief ally and adviser throughout.

Finally, thanks to John Brooks for his brilliant photography. The Jones and Newman families for their love, support, and courage. And, of course, LeAlan and Lloyd.

—David Isay

Thanks to my grandmother, my mother, unknown father, grandfather, sisters, uncles and aunties, cousins, and my nephew Muckie. Thanks also to Earl B. King, president of the No Dope Express Foundation, Darryl King and Little Earl, and the Smith family, Reverend Leon Perry and the Metropolitan Community Church, Coach Lonnie Williams and the Martin Luther King High School football team, Dr. Richard Smith, the students and faculty at King (especially the class of '97), the Chicago Teacher's Union, the Board of Education (especially the staff at Vocational Education), ETHS, Chris Breckenridge, Rashad Haynes, the CREI Organization, Evanston Township High School, Mark Larson and the class of '97, Robert Blackwell, Jeff Carter, Anna

ACKNOWLEDGMENTS

Simms-Phillips, Alvin and Aaron Collins, Darren Collins, Jeffrey New-ing, Rudolph and Terrence Jones and all my family in St. Louis and Detroit, my cousins the Raspberries, the Mixon family, Steve Miller, Robe Imbriano, Adam Mosston, Sandy Delamberte, Patsy Palmer, Harold Dahlstrand of Speigel, the Wynn family, Dr. Bobby Austin of the W. K. Kellog Foundation, the National African-American Leadership Summit, the National African-American Male Collaboration, and the Center for Inner-City Studies. I want to thank everyone in the Ida B. Wells who supported us and gave us encouragement while we were working. I love you all and stay strong! Thanks to John Brooks, and special thanks to Lloyd Newman and David Isay—my partners. Much love, and if I missed you, it wasn't on purpose!

—LeAlan Jones

I want to give thanks to Diana, Sophia, Erica, Lyndell, my brother Mike, and my nephew and niece. I want to give thanks to all the residents of the Ida B. Wells. Also thanks to Gary Covino, Rick Karr, and all the other people who helped us put the radio pieces together. Thanks to John Brooks and to my partner, LeAlan Jones, for aid and assistance. I want to thank my mother for living long enough to teach me what I know. And most of all I would like to give thanks to Dave Isay for bringing this all together.

—Lloyd Newman

I would first like to thank God. Thanks also to my parents, Diana Brooks and Charles Bracey, and my mentor, Tom Maday—these three people made me what I am today. Thanks to my wife, Sahara Newby Brooks, who puts up with me every day, my two kids, Colby and Elijah, my two brothers, Charles and Jermaine, and my best friend, Melvina Nunn. Thanks also to Cheryl, Victor, and Mary at Gallery 37, Sam Landers, Star, Batya Goldman, James Whitehead, Project Match, Demico Youth Center, New Expressions, and Cabrini. I cannot forget my boyz, Durvile, Bruce, Cornbread, and Randy—keep it real. To all my brothers and sisters who make it, please don't forget where you came from—we need you! Oh yeah—Dave, LeAlan, and Lloyd—peace!

—John Brooks

INTRODUCTION

In February 1993, my friend and mentor Gary Covino called and asked if I would be interested in contributing a documentary to a series he was editing for public radio station WBEZ in Chicago. The series was called *Chicago Matters*, and examined issues of race and ethnicity around the city. We kicked around the idea of trying to do something a little different—maybe giving people tape recorders and having them record their own stories. I had just finished reading Alex Kotlowitz's *There Are No Children Here*, which follows the lives of two brothers growing up in Chicago's Henry Horner Homes, and decided to model the documentary, in spirit, after his work. Kotlowitz spent several years with his subjects. I had enough funding for about a week's worth of recording.

I decided to spend seven days with young people growing up in Chicago public housing, to equip them with tape machines and have them compose diaries of their lives, sound portraits of growing up in poverty. Two kids—friends, brothers, sisters—it didn't matter. I'd hire them as reporters for a week and give them a chance to tell their stories.

I sent out letters to social service agencies and high schools all over Chicago asking for help in finding subjects: young people living in fairly typical circumstances who were atypically expressive and introspective. I received a lot of callbacks from agency heads, community activists, teachers, and social workers suggesting young people to work with. If they sounded promising, I'd ask to have the kids call me collect. I talked to a lot of good kids and a lot of people who cared about them a great deal. "The courage these kids show is incredible," one teacher told me. "Nobody's listened to these children for years. Who wants to listen to a poor child? But these kids want to talk. They want to tell their stories. I have twenty-eight kids, and twenty-eight hands shot up when I told them about this project. They all immediately started writing their autobiographies for you. They *all* want to be heard!" Tough choices.

About two weeks into my research I got a call from Earl B. King, who runs a Chicago anti-gang program called No Dope Express Foundation. He said he had a thirteen-year-old I might want to speak with named LeAlan Jones. LeAlan got on the phone and started talking. He talked a lot. He was a smart kid. I liked him. I asked if there was anyone else—a brother, a sister, a friend—whom he might want to work with. He called me collect that night from a pay phone in the Ida B. Wells (Chicago's oldest African-American public housing development) and said, "Here he is . . ." Another voice came on the line. He said his name was Lloyd, and he was about to turn fourteen. He was shy, with a sweet tone to his voice. Lloyd asked me some thoughtful questions about what I was up to. He said his mother had died, his father was an alcoholic, and his two sisters were raising him. "This kid's a heartbreaker," I jotted in my notes. Lloyd put LeAlan back on, and LeAlan put Lloyd back on. They goofed around. I was laughing. They were smart. They were funny. They were the ones.

I flew out to Chicago a week later. That first night I met with LeAlan and Lloyd in the living room of LeAlan's house and spent a couple of hours teaching the kids how to use their tape recorders. They picked it up quickly. We discussed whom they might interview and what questions they might ask. The next morning they were off. That afternoon they gave me their first batch of cassettes and headed out to record some more. I sat in my hotel room and listened. LeAlan's first tape began: "Good morning. Day 1. Walking to school. Leaving out the door . . . This is my walk every day, so I'm taking you on a little journey through my life. Yes, my life. Yeah . . ."

LeAlan and Lloyd recorded for a total of seven days. We each had beepers. They'd beep me when their tape recorders went on the fritz (once or twice a day); I'd beep them when I wanted to pick up cassettes. I spent the days listening to tapes and making notes. At night we would meet. I'd have them read the most recent transcripts of their recordings, give them notes, discuss any technical problems, talk about what they might do the next day. They would listen, shoot back with their own ideas, and try to end the meeting as quickly as possible so they could go play video games at the corner store.

It was a remarkable experience—sitting in my room in Chicago, listening to these stories unfold on tape. Day after day I was dumbfounded at the honesty, humor, and courage of the kids and their families. LeAlan and Lloyd were insightful, intensely curious, meticulous observers—a poignant mixture of little boys and adolescents wise far beyond their years. Every few days the kids would get on the bus and ride, "just to get a break from the ghetto," LeAlan told me. They'd talk nonstop. They had been doing it for years. LeAlan and Lloyd had discovered their own strategy for coping with the devastation all around them and staving off the boredom and depression: Mop it all up and discuss it endlessly. Break it down. Look at it from all the angles. Quiz each other for details. Collect information. Laugh about it sometimes. Don't let *anything* slip by unnoticed.

So maybe it's not so surprising that they took to the task of creating a snapshot of their lives with such confidence and ease. I'd give them interview questions, and they'd come up with their own (invariably more interesting than the ones I had suggested). The kids would make notes on their tape recorders as to how the piece should sound, what music should be used where, which scenes they liked and which they didn't. Early on, LeAlan switched on his tape recorder and said that he'd come up with a name for the documentary: *Ghetto Life 101*. So it was.

The kids recorded the documentary in early March 1993. I cut the documentary in New York, playing sections of it for LeAlan and Lloyd over the phone. I drafted a script, basing it largely on diary entries LeAlan had made on his tape recorder before going to sleep. We revised it together. The boys recorded their narration in Chicago, and I mixed the piece in New York.

Ghetto Life 101 premiered on WBEZ in Chicago in May 1993 and was broadcast nationally on NPR's *All Things Considered* in early June. The documentary generated a small avalanche of listener and press accolades, as well as some controversy (most of which revolved around issues of a white producer working with African-American kids). It won more than a dozen national and international awards, including the Prix Italia, Europe's oldest and most prestigious broadcasting honor. That was the kids' favorite—probably because of the $10,000 prize we split three ways (as we did with all money generated by the production). *Ghetto Life 101* was translated into several languages and broadcast worldwide.

Jump ahead a couple of years. The boys and I remained close, talking on the phone several times a week. One evening in October 1994, I got a call from LeAlan: "A shorty [a little boy] just fell out the window behind my house." A day later I saw the story in *The New York Times:* five-year-old Eric Morse was dropped out of a fourteenth-floor window in the Ida B. Wells by two other boys—ten and eleven years old. LeAlan, Lloyd, and I talked about the incident. We hadn't intended to collaborate on another radio documentary, but this seemed like a particularly important and appropriate story for the boys to cover. After kicking it around for a couple of months, we decided to go ahead with the piece.

LeAlan and Lloyd spent about a year recording the story (through most of 1995). Over the course of their investigations, they became the nation's experts on a tragedy which made headlines across the country when the two boys convicted of the crime became the youngest kids ever sentenced to prison in this country.

LeAlan and Lloyd named this documentary *Remorse: The 14 Stories of Eric Morse.* They decided to score this piece with jazz music, instead of rap as with *Ghetto Life* ("maturing sensibilities," explained LeAlan), and we enlisted the help of the great alto saxophonist Frank Morgan. When Morgan released his debut album, *Introducing Frank Morgan,* in 1955, he was hailed as the next Charlie Parker. Soon after, a heroin addiction landed Morgan in the penitentiary, where he spent most of the next thirty years. Morgan was assumed dead by most jazz fans until the mid-1980s, when he straightened out and began recording again. Since 1985 Morgan has put out a dozen first-rate albums. We were inspired by Morgan's story, and felt his work appropriate to score *Remorse.*

The documentary premiered on *All Things Considered* in March 1996. It was the first hour-long feature broadcast on the show since 1981. Listener response was overwhelming. LeAlan was sixteen and Lloyd had just turned seventeen when it aired.

INTRODUCTION

And now the final part of this trilogy: *Our America*. The boys had recorded a little more than fifty hours of tape for each of their two radio documentaries, the vast majority of which was not broadcast because of unintelligibility, technical problems, and (most of all) the time constraints of radio. For years now the raw tapes from *Ghetto Life 101* had sat on a shelf next to my desk, nagging me. I knew there was a wealth of powerful words on these cassettes that needed to be heard: interviews, monologues, and moments that would add new depth and dimension to LeAlan's and Lloyd's stories. I was left with the same feeling after finishing our second documentary. Soon after storing the raw tapes from *Remorse* on the shelf just below *Ghetto Life*, we were approached to write this book.

We put *Our America* together during the summer and fall of 1996. The first two sections are drawn from interviews, monologues, and conversations collected for *Ghetto Life 101* and *Remorse* (although a couple of interviews included in "Death—1995" were conducted after the completion of the radio documentary). The words are all LeAlan's and Lloyd's. I did the sequencing and editing with steady input from the boys.

For the book's epilogue, "Life—1996," LeAlan and Lloyd conducted some new interviews and revisited some of the people they encountered when recording *Ghetto Life 101*. While doing this work, the boys were accompanied by a young self-taught photographer named John Brooks. We found John through Gallery 37, a jobs program for inner-city Chicago kids interested in the arts. John's intimate black-and-white portraits of his family, friends, and neighbors from Cabrini Green won us over immediately. He was a natural to join the team.

From the beginning of this project it has been my intention to act as the vehicle through which the voices of young people growing up in poverty might reach a larger public. Over the past twenty-five years conditions in this nation's ghettos have been deteriorating steadily. With the loss of urban manufacturing jobs and the exodus of all but the most deeply disadvantaged residents, neighborhoods like the Ida B. Wells have become increasingly isolated, impoverished, and dangerous. There is little or no work. The odds of making it out are slim. Communities are sealed behind invisible fences; residents are consigned to live in high-rise bunkers of wire mesh and boarded-up windows.

INTRODUCTION

It's my hope that this work might help begin to tear some holes in these fences, allowing the rest of the country to meet a few of the people who live behind them. Magnificent people blessed with the remarkable human capacity to adapt to the bleakest of circumstances.

As we finish putting *Our America* together, I'm astonished once again by what LeAlan, Lloyd, and John have accomplished. They are, without question, remarkable young men. But they are remarkable kids growing up around many other kids who *didn't* get the opportunity to tell their stories. I'd like to think that *Our America* stands as a testament to the potential of *all* of these young people. As another reminder that behind the walls of poverty and neglect live real children who laugh and struggle and dream and hurt and love. There's a saying that keeps coming to mind: Just give a kid *something*—a microphone (or a camera, or a paintbrush, or a computer), and watch what he can do. Watch what he can do.

—David Isay
November 1996

AUTHOR'S NOTE

Our America was edited from more than a hundred hours of tape recorded by LeAlan and Lloyd. Some of the language, grammar, and slang in the interviews have been corrected to make for easier reading. A number of names have also been changed to protect the identities of minors and others who do not wish to be identified. All references to gangs and gang members have been omitted for the safety of LeAlan, Lloyd, and their families.

LeAlan did most of the talking on the tapes from which this book was written (he is an extraordinarily gifted speaker), with Lloyd listening hard by his side, curious and admiring, every so often tossing in a wide-eyed question or comment. Except for the chapters on Lloyd's life, *Our America* is in LeAlan's voice.

—D. I.

A GHETTO GLOSSARY

Booster: Someone who steals out of stores and resells the merchandise at an 80 percent discount.

Crib: Home. Where you live.

Darrow Homes: The four high-rise buildings in the Ida B. Wells.

Def Homes: Darrow Homes. Our nickname for the Ida B. Wells high-rises.

Dummy bag: Fake drugs—like baking powder.

Ends: Money, loot.

Flip: Do gymnastics, usually on an old mattress. A favorite activity for shorties in the 'hood.

Hype: Crack fiend. Willing to sell anything to get drugs.

Ida Bees: Ida B. Wells development.

Kicking it: Hanging out.

Light up: Shoot someone.

Nine: Nine-millimeter (Glock) gun.

Player: Buddy. Dude. Someone who's cool.

Pop: Shoot.

Pushing keys: Serving kilos of cocaine.

Ready, ready rocks: Rock cocaine.

Rep: Reputation.

Serving: Selling drugs.

Shorty: Young one.

Smoke: To murder.

3833: 3833 South Langley, the address of the building where Eric Morse was killed in the Darrow Homes.

Tripping: Crazy. Out of your mind.

The Wells: Ida B. Wells development.

This is our second language. It's the way we communicate with the people that we live around.

PART I

LIFE—1993

LeAlan (left) and Lloyd, 1993

CHAPTER 1

THE BEGINNING

LeAlan: My name is LeAlan Jones, I am thirteen years old, and I live with my family in a house around the corner from the Ida B. Wells.

Lloyd: My name is Lloyd Newman, I am just fourteen years old and I live in a row house in the Ida B. Wells.

LeAlan: We've been friends since first grade. That's seven years of our life! That's a long time growing up in this community together!

Lloyd: I don't even remember the first time we met. . . .

LeAlan: . . . I remember. It was in the first grade. Not on the first day of school. It was on the second day.

Lloyd: But we started really hanging out about three years ago. I mean *really* started hanging out.

LeAlan: We were best friends, but we didn't hang out, 'cause Lloyd lives in The Wells and they used to shoot a lot, so my momma didn't really allow me to go over there. We used to talk in school, but when 2:30 was up, I didn't see him till the next morning on the breakfast line. I used to be scared walking home from Lloyd's house, because the field that I had to walk through is just an open area and you can't get behind anything if they start shooting. A lot of people got shot there.

Lloyd: Like one time, LeAlan was ready to leave my house, and I said, "Stay for a little more while." And if he would have left any earlier he would have gotten shot, because they had a shoot-out in that field.

The Field Between Our Houses

LeAlan: They used to shoot a lot in the summertime. It seems like when I was little I can't hardly remember the wintertime, but the summertime—I can remember the summertime! It was dangerous, but it was fun.

Lloyd: We used to play It. . . .

LeAlan: Then when you hear bullet shots you would duck. . . .

Lloyd: And run in the house. . . .

LeAlan: And look outside. Go outside again, then POP! POP! POP! POP! Go on back in the house again.

Lloyd: That's all you could do all day!

LeAlan. It's like running the marathon!

Lloyd: That's why I stayed in my house most of the time.

LeAlan: Let me describe Lloyd. He's short. Weighs about seventy-five pounds. He's so skinny that I have an inch around my finger when I put it around his wrist. He got a head like a Martian—his head takes up about sixty percent of his natural body weight! Could you talk about me now?

Lloyd: All right. LeAlan is short. His belly takes up his whole body— about one hundred percent of his natural body weight (really, he needs to go to Belly Busters)! We call him Bucky Rogers because of his beaver teeth—they hang all the way down to his chin! If something ever happens to Woody Woodpecker, they know LeAlan's address!

LeAlan: Lloyd's silly, but he's smart. He knows math better than me, and I know reading better than him, so we help each other out. . . .

Lloyd: If he's in a fight and he's losing, I'm gonna jump in . . .

LeAlan: And if I find something, me and Lloyd will split it. We share things. Equally share.

Lloyd: I like the way we treat each other!

Filth in the Ida B. Wells

CHAPTER 2

THE 'HOOD

Our neighborhood is a fun neighborhood if you know what you're doing. If you act like a little kid in this neighborhood, you're not gonna last too long. 'Cause if you play childish games in the ghetto, you're gonna find a childish bullet in your childish brain. If you live in the ghetto, when you're ten you know everything you're not supposed to know. When I was ten I knew where drugs came from. I knew about every different kind of gun. I knew about sex. I was a kid in age but my mind had the reality of a grown-up, 'cause I seen these things every day!

Like when I was eight years old, my cousin Willy had a friend named Baby Tony and another friend, Little Cecil. They used to hang out—watch TV, go to the park and hoop, sell drugs. They all went to jail. When Baby Tony came out he was walking through the park when a boy lit him up and blew his face off. His face was *entirely* blown off. And then a couple of days later Little Cecil sold somebody a dummy bag of plaster from off the walls, so the man who was using it came back and asked him for his money back. Little Cecil took off running and the man shot him. And Cecil was dead. That was both of my cousin's friends that died in one week! And I heard about this when I was *eight!* I had just seen Baby Tony the day before he died.

It's like Vietnam. I remember one time I was over at my auntie's house spending the night. We were playing Super Nintendo and I heard this lady say, "I heard you been looking for me, nigger!" Then she just—BOOM! BOOM! BOOM! BOOM! She let off about eight

Playing in Shopping Carts

Shorties Hanging Out

shots. Then I heard the other gun fire off. And we were just still there playing like nothing happened. In Vietnam, them people came back crazy. I live in Vietnam, so what you think I'm gonna be if I live in it and they just went and visited? Living around here is depressing! It's depressing! Just look outside—this isn't Wally and the Beaver!

•   •   •

It's Friday afternoon after school, and we're going to take you on a tour of our neighborhood. It's about sixty degrees today—feels good out. Walking down the streets. See an abandoned building, graffiti on the wall. See some little kids playing on a little shopping cart that they got from Jewel Supermarket.

Walking by some abandoned houses—looks like some Scud missiles just bombed them out. A lot of trash here—glass and things. Used to be little snakes in this field in the summertime and we'd catch them. People out here pitching pennies. Houses boarded up.

Walking through puddles of water. Bums on the street. An abandoned church. A helicopter. There goes somebody we thought was dead—guess he ain't dead.

By the old library, which is no longer in business—there was a murder in there last year and they closed it down. See a "Rest in Peace" sign. Birds flying. There's the store that they burned down when the Bulls won the championship. Going by the gas station where they sell liquor and food. Now we see some spray paint that says: "Justice for Rodney King/Revolution Is the Only Solution."

Now we're walking in the Ida Bees, which is 50 percent boarded up. Now we're by Lloyd's house. Abandoned apartments. Broke-down basketball hoops. We see little kids just sitting around looking at us.

Now we're walking in the parking lot where they play loud music in the summertime. Little trees growing up in the concrete cracks. See a trash Dumpster and graffiti. See an airplane overhead. A bum walking down the street. We're walking through the ghetto. Our neighborhood.

CHAPTER 3

SCHOOL

We're both in eighth grade at Donoghue Elementary School, fixing to graduate in a couple of months. There are twenty-eight kids in our homeroom class, and it's pretty rowdy most of the time.

But in our classes we're a bunch of smart kids! If you could just hear some of the things we talk about—ooh, we have some heavy discussions! We talk about the government. We talk about the President, what Bush is doing when the cameras aren't around, how JFK got assassinated, what they did to Mike Tyson, and how William Kennedy Smith got off. We've always been doing that—since third grade. Man, it might not look like it, but we read the newspapers. We're smart kids!

Ms. Margaret A. Tolson has been the principal at Donoghue since 1991. We interviewed her in the front office about her job and our school.

Is it hard being a principal in this neighborhood?
Ms. Tolson: Yes, it's difficult. Not so much because the children are really any different. It's difficult because of the publicity that surrounds our housing development and community. People set their minds, before they come here, to expect problems, and generally you get what you expect. There *is* danger in and around the school. You all live in it every day. That means if we work here, we work in it. So that

Ms. Tolson

makes it difficult. And we have difficulty convincing you that we believe in you, that we don't believe that you will grow up to be members of gangs, that you can achieve anything that you want to achieve. We have to convince you of that every day. And you don't believe that we believe you're smart.

So it's very difficult. It's difficult for some teachers to see the skills that you have. But one of the reasons I'm here is to help to train teachers to look at the gifts that you bring with you. Many of you get up in the morning, deal with whether or not an elevator is working, you may dress a brother or sister, may stop at the store to get some breakfast. Those are all skills that can be used in education. But it's a matter of showing you that it is a skill. Many of you cook, and you cook quite well considering what you use to create meals. We can use the measurements in math, we can use labels in reading. But it's a matter of training a teacher so that she can pull all of that out of you and use it for education. So yes, it's difficult. But can it be done? Sure.

LeAlan: *Do you see any gang activities here that you would see in the movies like* **West Side Story***?*
At times, yes. I know that I have some gang members. But they come to school and many of them try to be halfway respectful while they're here.

You all have a decision to make about gangs, whether or not it's going to be a part of your life. I hope it won't. But I also hoped that you wouldn't see the guns and the shootings. But have you experienced it? Yes. We have children who have been killed. We have children who have been shot on the street in front of school. As a matter of fact, the first summer that I arrived, within the first week we had a drive-by shooting at the front door. Then we had another drive-by shooting within two days that started over near your house, Lloyd. I sent you all out the back door that day. So yes, we've seen some of the things like you see in the movies. Do they happen every day? No.

LeAlan: *Do you hear kids talk about some of the things they see that you didn't see at a young age?*
Oh yes. I have some of my students who know more about gangs, guns, and sex than I do, because they have observed things. I have kindergartners who can tell you about sexual intercourse, who can tell

you about guns and gangs, but cannot read and have not found a great many things in their life enjoyable. I would hope that none of you would have to see a family member get shot in front of you, but I know I have plenty of students who have seen that. I would hope that none of you would have to experience having hepatitis or AIDS. But I know that I have students who have to deal with that. They know about a lot of things I would wish they would never see.

Lloyd: *Ms. Margaret A. Tolson, what does the "A" stand for in your name?*
Armstrong. It's my middle name.

Lloyd: *Could you describe us?*
Let me see. . . . Lloyd. Lloyd is a quiet young man in school who could do a lot more things if he would believe in himself. He should speak up a little more often about his ideas, because Lloyd has a lot of ideas and a lot of things that he is capable of doing.
LeAlan is a very expressive young man. He has opinions about things. He thinks in depth. He takes a look at situations around him. He observes carefully. You challenge things, which is good. You will listen to someone else's side but you won't necessarily accept it.

Lloyd: *What do you think we'll be when we grow up?*
LeAlan will be a politician. Lloyd, I think you will be behind the scenes—probably a businessman and a millionaire and I'll have to come borrow money from you in my old age.

Lloyd: *Are there any classes that you call the baddest class in Donoghue?*
No. Now, are my eighth graders my most rambunctious group? Yes. You all keep me challenged every day, to say the least.

Lloyd: *What do you think of the people in eighth grade? What will they become in life?*
Well, if they're true to form for Donoghue, they will become politicians, lawyers, judges, doctors, secretaries, teachers in the classrooms at Donoghue. They will become expert workmen, technicians—most anything that they want to become.

Lloyd: *Mrs. Tolson, what percentage of the students do you think are going to fall down?*
How many are not going to make it? I'd say maybe about five to six percent.

•　　•　　•

One day my buddy Stevie grabbed my mike and started goofing. He did a whole fake radio broadcast pretending he was David Duke:

Stevie: (pretending he's David Duke): I'm your host, David Duke, the host of this show, *The Lifestyles of the Nice and White*. We're just going to talk about how much I hate niggers. See, all niggers deserve to die. Want a good way to kill a nigger? You tie him to a tree and pour hot tar all over him, or you get a knife and cut all the way up to his throat, or you can just lynch the guy real tight around the neck until his head pops open. That's forty good ways to kill a nigger. I'm your host David Duke.

One day me and my friend J. Edgar Hoover were walking through the woods, and a black man came up and said, "Hey, white man, what are you doing in our territory? This is black man's territory!" And we said, "This is our land, nigger, we brought you here. . . ." Then the niggers started throwing rocks at us. So I did my Klansman call and Klansmen started coming out of the sewers and out of the trees. The niggers started running. And we said, "Now we got you!" And started shooting. Winchester rifles. And we just blew their brains out. Two of them got away, but we caught them later on. We dragged one of them out of his house, put him on a cross, and burned his black ass crisp! The other one? Had to use the bloodhounds. Very good dogs! We caught that nigger in Harlem, tied him to a tree, poured hot tar all over him, stuck a match in his ass, and cut out his esophagus. Then we lynched that black motherfucker. That's one way to kill a nigger. Remember: you can never trust a nigger, because niggers aren't trustworthy, O.K.? I'm your host, David Duke, signing off.

•　　•　　•

If you take a kid from a suburban area, no matter what race, and you take a kid from a ghetto area, who sees the things that people do to survive—I mean the raw things: steal, shoot, kill, shoot drugs to get a high; and the kid in the suburban area who has people who live in nice

41

Ghetto Kids

homes, washrooms work, doesn't have to worry about anyone breaking in all the time, not hearing shooting every day. If you put those two together, you'll see a dramatic difference. The ghetto kid's going to be hostile and gangster-like. He'll be more angry. He'll get more frustrated. And the suburban kid will be sensitive and talk his way out of things. He'll be more skillful at things like how to get a job. He'll be more into his books.

But then sometimes the suburban kid (there's a history to this!) doesn't have to work and gets everything he wants. That's why you see a lot more suicides committed in the suburban area—because the suburban kid doesn't have to work for nothing and he just goes crazy! The ghetto kid always has to work. And I'd rather work for something than be born with a silver spoon in my mouth any day!

There's no kids from around here that we know who are really doing O.K. in school past the second or third grade. But I bet if you take anybody from Donoghue out of this environment and put them in a suburban school, boy, they're going to hear some things they never heard of and think of some theories they never thought of. If you take them out of hearing gun shots every day—POP! POP! POP!—if you get 'em out of Vietnam-listening every day, every night, and every second, you're going to see a big difference. These kids around here are looking at life from the inside out and not from the outside in, 'cause if they were looking from the outside in, they would see what they're doing and know that it's wrong.

·   ·   ·

After school one day I saw George from our class hanging out on the street selling drugs. He hadn't been to school for about three weeks and looked like a bum. Made me mad! I caught up to him, and this was our conversation:

Man, why you ain't been to school?
George: School ain't shit.

How you gonna be something if you don't go to school?
You ain't learning shit now, so why? Why?

The Neighborhood Store

SCHOOL

You ain't learning shit out here. I bet I'm gonna see your ass twenty-five years from now begging for a quarter so you could get a drink!
I ain't gonna be alive in ten years because I'll be selling my drugs and they're gonna pop my ass. No one's gonna be alive in twenty more years!

I'm gonna be alive! I know I am!
Your ass ain't gonna be alive in ten years!

George just turned his back and walked away from me. Made me so mad! Out here selling drugs, talking about how "school ain't shit." I guess he wants to be like that for the rest of his life. Motherfucking drug dealer!

The View fom the Bridge over Lake Shore Drive

CHAPTER 4

KICKING IT

Growing up in the ghetto is fun, but it's dangerous. Sometimes it can be boring, and when we're bored we do some crazy things to pass the time—like throwing rocks at cars. We go to the bridge over Lakeshore Drive, wait until the car gets close, and just drop it—BAM! And the windshield might crack or something. And you can see them in their car—they might pull over and get out and look at you. I don't care about those people—they're going to the suburbs. What are they gonna do? Get out and chase us? I'd like to see if they have enough heart to come in the projects . . . And if somebody did come in the projects, I'm not racist or anything, but if he's white I don't got to touch you. My associates will take care of that. That's the enjoyment of the projects.

Other times we just walk on over to the lakefront, sit on the rocks, and kick it:

LeAlan: Isn't this a pretty view?
Lloyd: Love it!
LeAlan: I could sit here all day, man. Just sit here and talk. Let the wind hit the grass. It's what we used to do when we were little.
Lloyd: How far do you think you could swim?
LeAlan: Not that far. Do you think you could keep swimming and swimming?

Lloyd: Maybe for a hundred million dollars.

LeAlan: I'd be scared. . . .

Lloyd: You could swim about to right there—I'll throw a rock in to show you how far. If you keep swimming straight, where you think you'd end up at?

LeAlan: You'd have to float for maybe a week before you get to Milwaukee or Toronto.

Lloyd: Feel that cool breeze?

LeAlan: A nice little breeze going. Clear blue sky. It's a good day today. Good time to reminisce. This is a Kodak moment, sitting here.

Lloyd: Hey, LeAlan, if you saw a nuclear bomb fly past us and you knew it was gonna land in Chicago, what would you do?

LeAlan: If it was flying right over our heads and I saw it was fixing to hit something? I'd jump under the water.

Lloyd: If you went under the water you think you would feel it?

LeAlan: I'd be boiling like a chicken!

Lloyd: You think you'd die?

LeAlan: Either I'd drown or burn to death.

Lloyd: How long do you think a nuclear bomb would last?

LeAlan: The effects of it? A hundred years. Man, you think if you was in that airplane right there and you jumped out into the water you'd survive?

Lloyd: Yeah. If you don't die before you hit the water. . . .

LeAlan: But you'd be hurt. You got to be in some deep, deep, deep water to survive!

Lloyd: Would you jump out of that plane with an umbrella for a hundred million dollars?

LeAlan: Hell no! I ain't Mary Poppins!

Lloyd: We talk every day, don't we?

LeAlan: Yup.

Lloyd: Helicopter just flew by. . . .

LeAlan: In Vietnam, they had cannons on the helicopters. They could blow that building down. Man, I bet you I could shoot that vacant apartment over there.

Lloyd: With a scope. . . .

LeAlan: I don't need a scope. Just get me a rifle. I could hit anybody in any of these cars—I got aim! I bet I could snipe anybody!

Lloyd: How far do you think a bullet could go from right here?

LeAlan: With a high-powered rifle, that bullet could go a thousand yards. I could hit anybody in the Darrow Homes. I could take anyone out. . . . Man, it's beautiful out here! Good time to reminisce! I'm thinking about that time I cut my grandmother's coat up when I was five. She had some scissors, right?

Lloyd: You were trying to fix it?

LeAlan: No, no. I saw on the TV where they were doing some surgery. She had just bought the coat, and I took the scissors and I went over there and shredded it. When she woke up—I still remember that whupping! She said, "Come here, boy!" Much as I wanted to run, I had to walk to her, because if I didn't, it meant another minute with that belt. One time I called the police: "My momma just beat me! My momma just beat me!"

Lloyd: I'm glad it ain't like the old days. . . .

LeAlan: When she'd say, "I'm gonna give you the best whuppin' you ever had". . .

Lloyd: And you're crying for about ten minutes, and you can't stop. . . .

LeAlan: Then I'd cry myself to sleep. Soon as I wake up, Momma is right in front of my face with a big smile. I remember I tried to run away a couple of years ago after a beating. . . .

Lloyd: You were watching too much TV!

LeAlan: Yeah, man. I was fixing to sleep in a little ditch.

Lloyd: Where'd you go?

LeAlan: It was cold. There was an abandoned house. I went in, put newspapers over me like I was a bum, and went to sleep.

Lloyd: What did your grandma say when you got back?

LeAlan: I just went upstairs, started talking and laughing and everything was straight. I went downstairs, watched *Sanford and Son*, and went to sleep. That was the best sleep I ever had!

June Marie Jones

CHAPTER 5

LeALAN

Let me see. . . . First of all, I'm thirteen, but a lot of people think by the way I carry myself that I'm above my age. I'm an active person—I play football, basketball, and baseball. I'm a good student—I have a 9.4 grade level in reading. But most of all I talk a lot (as you can see, or else I wouldn't be doing this!).

I live in a house right around the corner from the Ida B. Wells. My grandmother, June Marie Jones, moved into the house back in 1937, and she's still here. We all live here—my grandmother, my grandfather, Gusie Jones, my mother (who's also named June but we call her Tootchie), my older sister, Janell, and her baby, Muckie, my younger sister, Jeri, and my cousin, Jermaine. My grandmother has custody of me and my sisters because my mother has a mental illness.

I interviewed my grandma on her bed late at night. My grandfather, who had two strokes and still didn't talk too much, was lying near by.

Hello. This is still Day 2. I'm on Tape 6. It's 12:06 in the morning. Fixing to interview my grandmother. Hello.
Grandma: Hello.

What are we going to talk about tonight?
We're going to talk about the neighborhood. How it has changed.

How do you think it's changed?
For the worse. I've been living in this area for over forty years, and I've seen a lot of changes: different types of people, different activities that the people do. When we first came in the area there were no projects—it was all homes. And this block was beautiful. You could stand at one end and look toward the other, and the trees would meet in the middle of the street. And at one time we had nice hotels where different movie stars would come and stay, and up on Pershing Road they had a lot of entertainment spots—it was almost like going downtown with all the bright lights. We had the Savoy, where the children could go roller skating; the Regal, where you would see live entertainment. There was some fighting, but not like it is now.

When did you start seeing a major change in the neighborhood?
It wasn't all of a sudden, it happened gradually. Day by day, year by year. I think one of the biggest things was when they made the high-rise homes in the neighborhood and stacked all of the people on top of each other. Ida B. Wells wasn't so bad before that—used to be beautiful. The people had beautiful yards, and took care of the houses. But the high-rises in the neighborhood brought in all types of people that just didn't take care of things like they should have.

What type of child was I was young?
You were a nice little red-headed boy with blue eyes.

I had blue eyes or brown eyes?
They were blue. They was lighter when you were young, and your hair was lighter. And it would turn white in the summer and darker in the fall.

How was I named?
You get your name from your two oldest uncles. The oldest boy's name was Alan and the second boy was Eric Lee, and your mother made your name out of the two names.

My name is LeAlan Marvin Jones. . . .
And she gave you the name Marvin. . . .

For Marvin Gaye. . . .
Because she liked to hear him sing.

My name is sentimental. I hold that dear to my name.
Yes. Your name is special, and you're a special person too.

How many kids do you have?
I had eight of them. Two of them are dead, so now I have six—three boys and three girls. The youngest one is twenty-nine and the oldest one is forty-three.

Which one would you consider your favorite child?
I don't have a favorite child. They're all the same—spoiled rotten—and so are the grandchildren. Especially you!

Get you! I've been waiting for thirteen years to get spoiled!
You're spoiled! Just like all the rest of them. You think you're supposed to get everything you want!

O.K. When did you have your first child?
In 1947. That was Alan. He died of Hodgkin's disease. The second was Judy, and the third was Baby Lee.

How did Baby Lee get murdered?
Baby Lee and his friend got in a argument, and his friend took the broken neck off of a beer bottle, and stabbed him in his leg. It hit the femoral artery and he bled to death. He was a good boy, but he liked to gamble and drink and run his mouth—just like his daddy.

Why do you think some of your kids got involved in drugs and alcohol?
Well, one reason, I guess, is because they wanted to. And then peer pressure has a lot to do with what people do—their friends was doing it, so they felt that they would try it out too. And I guess they liked it, so they kept on doing it.

Do you think they should have been more spectacular?
No. I think they each had a right to live their life the way they chose.

Those that achieved more, I thank God for. I thank God for those who didn't, even though they still could have done a little better with their lives.

Tell me about my mother's mental illness.
Well, when it first started they said she was a manic-depressive. Now they've changed it to bipolar. The state said they would put you all up for adoption because of your mother's mental condition, so rather than let the state take you and we would probably never get to see you again, I just told them I would take all three of you.

Do you know who my father is?
No, I do not.

Do you have a pretty good idea?
No.

Do you worry about me not having a father?
No, you seem to be doing all right. Even though it would be nice if you had a decent father.

Are you mad at Tootchie about this?
No. Are you? How do you feel about not having a father?

Same way you feel—I don't really care. I do fine. Probably would have been some deadweight anyway. Are you mad at Tootchie about this?
No, I'm not angry at her. It's because of her illness. I just feel that she was under medication at that time, and she might not even know herself who your father is. She might *think* she knows, but I doubt if she really knows herself who he is or where he is.

Do you think we've had it pretty hard?
No. When you look at other people's problems, ours aren't anything compared to theirs. I think I've been blessed, because things could have been a whole lot worse than they have been.

What career do you think I'll pursue?
Whatever it is, you'll be running your mouth. Maybe a lawyer. Might

be a preacher. I don't know. But whatever you do you'll be running your mouth like a bell clapper!

How do you think I'll end up?
I hope you end up with no drugs, well educated. And whatever you do with your life, do the best with it that you can. You might not be the tallest tree in the forest—you might just be a little shrub—but be the best shrub you can. Whatever you do, be the best. And I hope that you will.

• • •

One thing I think about almost every night is what it would be like if my grandmother died. Sometimes I have a dream that God calls her name, and I wake up and go upstairs just to see if she's still there. I might act bad around her and get mad at her, but deep down I love my grandmother. It's just that I can't show it. Telling someone you love them is soft, and if they see you're soft in the projects it's like a shark seeing blood—they're going to attack!

• • •

A couple of days later I interviewed my mother. Her name is also June Marie Jones, but everybody has always called her Tootchie. She's thirty-three years old and has three children—two girls and me.

What are some of your achievements in life?
Well, the first one . . . I was in eighth grade and I had a little speech to say at my graduation ceremony—I liked that. Then I worked for the government on several occasions, but lost the jobs due to illness. And having my children was an accomplishment.

What are you doing now?
I'm more or less recuperating from an illness. It's a slow recuperation, but when I feel better the doctor says that I can look for a position back with the government.

What do you think of your mother?
I think she's beautiful and well informed.

What are some of the things that she's done to really help you?
Taking custody of my children. Because if she wouldn't have took custody, I probably wouldn't have ever saw you again.

Tootchie Jones

Who is my father?
Your father is a fellow named Jack Johnson. He knows you exist. He seen you when you was about two. We were on Thirty-ninth Street, and your father drove up in his car with his family. He says, "Hey, how you doing?" I say, "I'm O.K." You were only two years old, and you had on that little coonskin hat with the fur around it and a little plaid jacket to match, and I said, "This is my son." And he didn't say nothing and just drove off. So the next time I seen him was in '84. I said, "Did I ever tell you that you had a son?" He said, "No." I said, "If I would have told you that you had one, would it make any difference?" He said, "No." And I ain't seen him since. What would you do if you saw your father?

Wouldn't do nothing. Just another man to me. I've lived half my life now. What do I need him for?
Not need him, but just know of him and see what he looks like?

Wouldn't care. Just another man to me. He ain't nothing to me. If he ain't been here thirteen years, what do I need him now for? I could die tomorrow and he still wouldn't know! Man, I'm fixing to graduate, fixing to go to high school. What I need him for? All I got is my grandparents, myself, you, and my sisters. That's all that I really hold dear to my heart. So he should be kicked to the curb so he can get run over by a bus. Hmmm . . .

If Jack was supposedly my daddy, why didn't you try to keep him around?
I did. I used to write him love letters.

In what ways do I favor him?
You got the color of his hair.

Do you feel bad about this?
I just feel it was God's will. It was already written when I was born what my life was going to be like.

How do you describe me? Do you see me as a little knot-headed kid or just a smart little know-it-all?
You're like a father—you act like somebody's daddy: "Turn off the TV!" "Change the radio dial!" "Don't take your medication with alcohol!"

You tell me about my clothes—"Why you wear them bell-bottoms?" You tell Jeri she needs to be quiet or Jermaine he's acting like a fool. And you tell me how I shouldn't give Janell my cigarettes.

What do you think I'm gonna be when I grow up?
A precinct captain, an alderman, a lawyer, or a United States representative, probably. Then if you live long enough you might make it to the Senate. You're outspoken. You like to talk.

Do you think that I'm a typical thirteen-year-old U.S. teenager?
I don't think you're typical, because a lot of people don't experience what you're experiencing and do positive things. I see you doing positive things.

Thank you.

•   •   •

Hello. It's LeAlan, and this is my diary. I'm talking to you from my bedroom. Really it's the living room and my bedroom. I ain't got no room—I sleep right here on this couch every night—and I'm fourteen almost. My mother is lying on the floor next to me on her little box spring, and my little sister's lying on the floor too.

I just interviewed my mom. She told me a lot of things about my father. It don't bother me. There's a lot of people out there without their own fathers. I ain't the only one. There's a couple of hundred thousand billion people around the world who don't know their fathers!

Let's see. . . . Went over to Lloyd's house after school today. We were watching this movie about this boy who was a booster. He got hit by a car and it knocked him out and he went back to slavery times. Back then the master beat you if you started to learn to read and write. This boy already knew, but he had to work in the cotton fields and pretend that he didn't. It made Lloyd's sister so angry and sad that she just started crying. That's why we have to fight for our education—because back then we had to fight and die just to read and write!

Sometimes when I'm watching TV I just wish I could dive through the screen and beat the hell out of people! Rodney King—when I see this, I get mad. Because this is nothing new to me—just beating the hell out of another nigger. I've seen police beat people in the street—beat 'em with fists and with bats. This time they caught it on film. So

58

what? It was a white man who did the recording. Who in the ghetto can afford a camcorder? If you put a camcorder in people's hands, I bet you'd see about fifteen Rodney Kings a day. This ain't nothing new to me!

To me, black people are just more friendly than white people. I see this every day on talk shows. You see a Ku Klux Klan man and a black man. The Ku Klux Klan man hates the black man's guts. But the black man always says, "I forgive you, man. I forgive you for your sins." But I'm not gonna stereotype the whole white race just for a few bigots. I know all white people can't be bad, 'cause God made us equal. We all of us human. We all got red blood. That's all for tonight. Signing off. Peace.

●　　　●　　　●

My older sister, Janell, is seventeen and lives in the room right across from my grandma. She has a little two-year-old baby named Jhery Marquis Jones, who we all call Muckie. Everybody in the house is worried about Janell. She's been messing up a lot lately. Just last week she drank so much E&J that she almost died—they had to take her to the hospital!

The way I see it, what's happening with Janell is like what's happened to a lot of kids in the neighborhood. A lot of times the girl who people say, "This is going to be the kid that makes it," is the first one to have babies. Or the boy who's into his books all day—all he really wants is to be "with it," so when he gets the opportunity he's going to do all kinds of bad stuff. But the kids that have always been doing bad stuff are going to be the ones to go to school, because they're already tired of living that way.

My sister is just like those "good" kids. She was in the spelling bee, she was in the Academic Olympics, she was the salutatorian of her class. Then she started hanging with these girls—their house was filthy, they were filthy—and they just kept dragging her down and down and down. She had a baby, started staying out of school, started coming home late. But she chose her own path—let her walk it. Eventually she's gonna see it ain't the right way.

I interviewed Janell in our front room:

Hey, Janell! Come here! Can I interview you?
Janell: I don't care.

Janell Jones

LeALAN

Hello, this is LeAlan Jones, sitting on the couch. It is 11:20. I'm gonna interview my sister, Janell Jones. Janell, tell me about yourself.
Well, I'm about five feet five in height. I weigh 116 pounds. I'm very fair-skinned. Um. . . . I'm very energetic, I like to have a lot of fun. . . .

Like to drink a lot. . . .
No, I don't.

Yes, you do. You smoke marijuana?
No, I don't.

Yes, you do! Tell the truth!
No, I don't!

Ummm. . . . Let me see. . . . You're seventeen?
Yes.

Have a child?
Yes.

How would your life be if your son wasn't here?
I probably would still be going to school. But I'm not saying that I regret having him, because I'd do it all over again. He's the most precious thing in my life. I love everybody in my family, but my baby is the most important thing to me right now.

When did you have him?
October the 10th, 1990.

Why did you name him Jhery Marquis Jones?
I don't know. . . . I guess Jeri was my little sister's name, so I changed the spelling for his name. And Marquis, I got that from my uncle Larry's car—he had a Grand Marquis.

By whom did you have this child?
Frankie Anderson.

How old was he at the time?
Sixteen.

What does he do for a living?
He doesn't have a job, if that's what you're asking.

What does he do?
I don't know what he do!

O.K. Where does Muckie's father live?
In the Ida B. Wells.

How did you meet him?
I used to go with a boy who was on the same basketball team that he was on. His name was Jermaine.

The one who got shot in the head?
Yeah. Jermaine got killed the same year I had my baby.

How did you feel about that?
I was sad. I was crying on the bus on the way home from the funeral.

How many close friends of yours have got killed through the years?
I don't know. I can't count all of 'em. . . . It's been a lot, though.

Could you name a few?
Like I said, Jermaine. And Yuk. Slick. Meatball. Cheezy and Vell. Shawn and Kenny. There's been a lot of people.

Would you say twenty-five?
Probably more than that. . . .

You think it was around fifty?
I don't think it was that many.

But around thirty or forty?
Probably somewhere in that area.

How do you feel about all these deaths when you just sit around and think about it?
Well, I know I didn't do nothing to nobody to make them do something to me, so I don't really have to worry too much.

For all the kids in America, what would you say to them about this?
About what? About killing? Well, there's a lot of people out there whose mommas just don't care. They don't give them money for nothing, and I feel if they have to sell drugs to get stuff that they need then they should be able to go ahead and do it. Now, I don't think it's right for them to go kill nobody, but I *do* think that the kids out there selling drugs should be able to do something to get them a little extra money. Because some of them might be too young to get a regular job at McDonald's. So that's what I think.

Thank you.

•   •   •

Yes, diary, this is me back again to give you my thoughts. Today we took our tests at school. Just sat in class all day writing. I don't like writing. I'm not going to be no Langston Hughes, and I'm not going to be no poet. I'm not a Plato or a Socrates or any of those people. I don't like writing—seriously! And if you don't like that, you can kiss my rumpadumpa.

Went on the West Side by the Bulls' stadium and showed Lloyd where my mother used to live in Henry Horner. I can remember when we used to visit her there on weekends when my grandmother first got custody of us. Sometimes we'd be sleeping and Momma would be fixing some popcorn. The train would go by, and we'd wake up and just start sniffing that popcorn like a rat smells cheese. We'd get up, go over to the next room, and sit up with her watching the late-night movie, eating that popcorn with hot sauce on it. It was fun!

My mother had lots of army men over there for me, and I would just sit playing all day. I had a setup: five squadrons, five men in front, five men in back, five men walking on the sides. I had a tank and an airplane that shot—BOP! BOP! BOP! BOP! BOP! I still like G.I. Joe men and things like that. I like airplanes and I like guns. I like talking about wars. That really interests me. Wars. Warfare. My mother could tell you that. I don't know in my past life what I could have been—probably was a war general, maybe in Egypt. Probably a person who led the chariots into battle or a person who strategized a war.

Sitting here thinking about my life. It ain't even halfway over yet, and I've already seen so much! [Yawn.] As you can hear, I'm very tired now, so I'm going to sign off. This is my diary, and I'll talk to you tomorrow. Peace out.

CHAPTER 6

LLOYD

I was born in Michael Reese Hospital on March 3, 1979, and lived in the Ida B. Wells all my life. I have two brothers: Mike is one year older, and Lindell is younger; and three sisters: Sophia and Precious are older, and Erica is younger. My mother died in 1991. She was thirty-five. I don't know the date, but I know she died in June.

Her name was Lynn Newman, and I think about her every night. I wasn't here when she died. Me and my brother Michael were selling papers downtown. Our boss, Lonnie, picked us up and told us to get in the van because he had some bad news. I said, "What?" He said: "First give me my money!" (He thought he wasn't gonna get his money if he told us the bad news first.) Then after we got through counting his money, he told us that our mother had died and he just drove us home real fast.

Sometimes at night I cry thinking about my mother—I stay under the covers so my brother won't know. When she was here I used to wake up in the middle of the night and go downstairs and just lay beside her, and we'd watch TV and laugh. Sometimes when I wake up, I think I see my momma standing right there before me. But now I have to get over it, because she's gone and I can't do nothing about it.

We live in a row house in the Ida Bees. It's pretty junky. The plaster's not fixed on the wall. No lightbulb in my room. Toilet been messed up since we been living here. About ten million roaches running all over everything—you see them crawling around now.

The View from Lloyd's House

My father drinks a lot—he's got a habit. So since my mother died, we've been raised up by my two sisters—Sophia and Precious. I couldn't believe the way Sophia and Precious took care of us when my momma died, because most teenagers would just worry about their boyfriends. I like what they're doing for us. My sisters are about all I have to look up to.

I talked to my sister Sophia in her bedroom:

How did Momma die?
Sophia: Well, she wasn't really drinking that much until after Grandma passed. She took that real hard. As soon as her mother died, she stopped eating, and started drinking more and getting real sick. One day her stomach was hurting real bad, and I told my cousin to call the ambulance. They said, "What's wrong with her?" and my cousin said, "Her stomach hurts." And they said it wasn't a good enough reason for them to come. So I said I would go with her to the hospital, and I went upstairs to pull on a pair of pants. My little sister came up and said Momma was on the floor, and I was like "Tell Momma to get up an' I'll be right down." My sister came back upstairs and said she wasn't responding. So I went downstairs and I saw vomit coming out of her mouth and her nose, and I ran for help. She was still breathing. We called the ambulance again, but there was a shooting right outside the door here, and the ambulance was fixing to drive off without my mother. My sister was crying, "My mother's still in there!" But the ambulance went anyway.

When we finally got to the hospital they were asking me all sorts of questions—"How old was your mother?" and "Who was her doctor?" And I thought that she was still alive until the doctor said the police would be out to talk to me. I knew then that she was dead. I took it real hard. They did the autopsy and they said cirrhosis of the liver. My mother was only thirty-five. Her birthday is January 27, and now my mother is thirty-seven.

First I just couldn't believe it. I was just like "How could you do this when you have six kids that love you? I know you cared about your mother, but how could you do this?" I was just so mad at her. And I was mad at God. And I stopped saying my prayers and everything because I was so mad. Then I realized my sister was six, and I said,

Precious (left) and Sophia Newman

"We got to do it. It's our responsibility now." Because my mother always said, "What are you going to do when I'm gone?" So it's rough, because being young, most girls would be like "Forget them!" and go party, but me and Precious are not like that.

What are your best memories of Momma?
Well, everyone said we looked just alike. But the best memories of all is how she loved all of us, and did everything she could for us. She never had a favorite child. And that's what I think about all the time—how great a mom she was. It keeps me from crying—'cause I used to cry all night. I just stopped crying in the last two months. On her birthday we remember her. Her birthday was January 27. Last year we celebrated. We had a cake and ice cream.

What about Chill?
Your father, his name is Michael Williams, but we call him Chilly—that's his nickname. We always thought he was gonna go before Momma. He was in the hospital for some months after she passed, going in and out of comas, and they didn't know if he was going to make it or not. But he made it. He stopped drinking for a couple of months, and we celebrated. We was proud of him. Now he's drinking again. Only time he drinks, he says, is when he thinks about my mother.

Do you think it's hard bringing us up at the age of twenty?
Well, I'll be twenty this year—I'm nineteen. I do think it's very hard, but I just ask for the Lord's help and go about it every day and try my best. Sometimes you all give us a tough time, but I love having you all as my brothers and sisters. We made it, and I'm very proud of us.

Do you call yourself a mother, raising us?
Yes. Sometimes people ask, "Do you got kids?" And I say, "Yeah, I got four of them. They're my brothers an' sisters, but I take care of them and I love them like they was my own!"

Thank you.

•   •   •

I love Chill, but he needs to stop drinking. Sometimes I'm embarrassed by him. Like when he wears my grandma's old red hat and he's

Chill

walking around and hollering and stuff. He did that yesterday. I felt embarrassed yesterday. And I'm embarrassed when he comes up to school sometimes. Like when I was in the spelling bee and got the word wrong and he's yelling, "Goddamn, boy! Why you miss that word?" And then the kids started laughing at him, and he told them to shut up. That made me embarrassed.

I interviewed my father in a car parked outside our house:

Michael Williams, why are you drinking?
Chill: I . . . I don't understand why I'm drinking. So many situations that I see makes me nervous. It's a worrisome world now. It ain't like it used to be. . . .

Do you think you're going to stop?
Yeah. I'm going into rehab and take care of myself so I can get back and deal with my children. I want my family back with me, 'cause I love 'em.

Why do you still drink?
Worrying about my family.

What do you drink?
I drink wine, about two or three pints of wine a day. But it ain't helping me, it's just killing me. It ain't doing nothing but destroying my body and destroying my family. Don't people understand it's destroying you?

If it's destroying you, why do you still drink?
That's why I got to go in the rehab program next week—because I don't want to destroy my family. I want my family.

What are your best memories of Momma?
Having fun. Sitting by the lake. Me and her putting our feet in the water together. Wasn't drinking, no drugs or nothing. Your mother loved me very good. She's the most beautiful woman I ever met. We were sober then. But once we started getting high, that memory is gone. They gone.

What do you think I'm gonna be when I grow up?
A good businessman, 'cause you know how to manage money. I showed you when you were a little small guy how to hustle on the street with me. I never would go out and stick nobody up, but I showed you who was the drug addicts, who was the wineheads, and don't go with different crowds. I used to give you little things to go hustle—laundry bags or whatever—and you'd go sell 'em and pocket the money. And everybody knew—that's my son!

Do you think you've been a good father?
Yes, I have. . . . To the best of my capability I could.

I have no further questions.

•   •   •

Chill comes over to our house every morning. Sometimes my sisters let him in, sometimes they don't. One day, when Chill was hanging out in our front room, he took my tape recorder and talked into the mike:

Chill: This is Lloyd's daddy talking. They call me Chilly. They gave me that name 'cause I was hustling—on the streets, shooting pool, craps, any kind of way I could get some money. Have shot drugs. Have been an alcoholic. Have been in clinics back and forth all my life.

But I don't know how it got like that, because I wasn't raised like that—I come from a good family. My father and my mother are the two greatest people in the world you would ever want to meet. My brother played professional baseball. My oldest sister is a teacher. I got another sister who works downtown. My other sisters have homes. If you ever got to know me, you'd know I'm a good fella. You meet my family, they're beautiful—especially my mother. She's seventy-six, and she loves me and I love her. But she sees what's going on in my life, and she do not like it. My sisters do not like it. My brothers do not like it.

I am the black sheep in the family. But people got to realize: The black sheep sees everything. He watches. He watches. I can see everything going on. One day I was down at Donoghue School, and I seen young boys snorting dope. Young boys. They had one of these record player albums, and they're scraping and mixing the dope right there on that album. And you can see them snorting—in Donoghue! They had a spelling bee contest. I was just sitting there trying to be a very proper father, but I'm hip to the game. I'm hip to it.

That's why I'm trying to get these children out of these projects. I'm an alcoholic, but I love my kids. I love Lloyd especially. He's a reporter now, and I love him for that. I want my son to grow up. I want my son out of this area. Soon as I get my family out of this neighborhood, they'll be a whole lot better.

I used to take Lloyd out selling laundry bags, you know. I sell laundry bags and socks and everything and Lloyd used to follow me everywhere I go, 'cause he knew his daddy would take care of him. I remember him running behind me, watching me hustle, making a little dollar there, a dollar here. He always watched me. I used to make him learn how to count his change. And I used to give Lloyd fifteen laundry bags, and I'd be sitting down in a barbershop somewhere talking to some old guys I know. He'd come in and say, "Daddy, I got a sale!" He made me so proud! He say, "Daddy," he smiled at me, he grinned, he say, "Daddy, you ain't got to do nothin' else. I made the money. It's time for us to go." We had some fond memories.

Please try to understand what I'm telling you. Listen to me. I'm sending a message: If you're on drugs and you have children, get into a rehab program and help your children before they get out there and be doing the same thing as you. You don't know what your kids are doing, 'cause you're too high to know. You might wake up one day, and somebody tells you your child is dead. Then what you gonna say? "My baby! My baby!" you gonna cry. "My baby, he's dead!" Then what you gonna do? Go buy some more dope. What does that solve? It's time for changes! Change has got to be made right now, before we destroy ourselves. We are destroying ourselves. 'Cause it's bad on these streets. It's pitiful out here.

That's why I'm gonna go into rehab—because I love my children. I love them. My old lady passed two years ago, and ever since then I don't know what's been happening with my life. It's time for me to make a move. Get back to the way I want to be, 'cause I'm scared. I love my kids. If I die and go to hell, who's going to help them?

This is Michael Williams speaking to you, Lloyd's father. Thank you and God bless you.

Mr. Johnson

CHAPTER 7

GHETTO GETAWAY

Lloyd: My favorite hobby is gambling: playing cards, craps—anything. I don't cheat—which everybody thinks I do since I always win all the money—I'm just lucky. Maybe when I'm losing I cheat sometimes—hide a card under my leg or something—but most of the time I just win. I'm hooked now. Once I start I can't stop.

LeAlan: Every week, there's a big card game at Lloyd's house, and most of the time he wins. Last night Lloyd won all the money again. Now we're fixing to get some breakfast food, since Lloyd got some ends. That's what we talk about with friendship—when Lloyd has some ends and I don't, he pays. Same thing when I got ends. That's friendship!

Lloyd: We're inside Johnson's Restaurant now. LeAlan just ordered everything on the menu. He eats more than anyone I ever met!

•   •   •

LeAlan: Just got finished eating.

Mr. Johnson: You all enjoy the meal?

LeAlan: Look at my plate.

Mr. Johnson: That didn't answer the question.

LeAlan: It was good!

Mr. Johnson: When I was your age, we didn't have milk. We had to put water in the cornflakes.

Lloyd: Water in the cornflakes?

Mr. Johnson: Water in the cornflakes. And powdered milk and powdered eggs.

75

LeAlan: Can we get a check?

Mr. Johnson: O.K. Sixteen dollars and twenty cents.

LeAlan: Can I get a receipt? Got to file my income taxes. Somebody's dependent on me.

[Everybody in Johnson's Restaurant laughs.]

Customer #1: Let me tell you something. I'm an accountant. Please don't try to file an income tax at your age. First question they gonna ask is where your income came from. What are you gonna tell them?

Customer #2: Ain't no goddamn way in the world you got no business spending sixteen-twenty on breakfast! So best thing to do is keep your mouth closed.

Mr. Johnson: Another thing you learn about growing up is you got to leave a tip. Ten percent. [Everybody laughs.] You want to eat big, you act big—leave a tip! It's really supposed to be fifteen percent, but it depends on how much you like me.

Lloyd: You gonna take out for the tip?

Mr. Johnson: No, that wouldn't be fair. We leave that up to your discretion. Your bill was sixteen-twenty. Ten percent of that is a dollar sixty.

LeAlan: You're not a dependent!

[Everyone laughs, and we leave a little tip.]

Mr. Johnson: All right, you all take it easy!

Lloyd: We just got through eating at Johnson's Restaurant.

LeAlan: I could eat again! My stomach's starting to get hungry!

Lloyd: You greedy, man!

LeAlan: I ain't greedy. After I burp, I bet you I'll be hungry again!

Lloyd: That's what I do, man! I'll be eating a big old food, and I just burp. . . .

LeAlan: And I'm starving again! I ate twelve French toasts, two omelets, and I was fixing to eat yours. . . .

Lloyd: That's all we do is eat, man—tell the truth, ain't it? Eat and talk!

•   •   •

After we left Johnson's Restaurant, we went to Funco Land to buy a Nintendo cartridge with the rest of the money Lloyd won. On the way out of Funco Land, we bumped into a shorty we never met before:

76

LeAlan: You fixing to buy a cartridge today?

Shorty: No, I'm trying to trade this cartridge in.

LeAlan: How old are you?

Shorty: Thirteen.

LeAlan: You in eighth grade?

Shorty: Seventh.

LeAlan: You fail?

Shorty: Once.

Lloyd: What's nine times nine?

Shorty: It's eighty-one.

Lloyd: Eleven times twelve?

Shorty: A hundred twenty.

Lloyd: Nope.

Shorty: A hundred twenty-two.

[Shorty notices Lloyd's beeper.]

Shorty: I got a Bravo at home.

Lloyd: What's a Bravo? A beeper?

Shorty: Yeah, a Bravo. I only break it out when my grandma goes somewhere.

LeAlan: What do you sell?

Shorty: Ready.

Lloyd: We're the police!

[We laugh.]

LeAlan: How you selling readies if you only thirteen?

Shorty: I be serving. I gang-bang.

LeAlan: Ain't nobody getting with readies no more, man! Who do readies?

Lloyd: And what are you supposed to do with it when you buy it?

Shorty: It's rocked-up cocaine. You boil the shit and it gets hard. You put it in cigarettes and smoke.

LeAlan: O.K., player, Shorty up on his. I don't know why you serving, though.

Shorty: Gotta get my money.

LeAlan: Does your momma know you serve?

Shorty: Never will know.

LeAlan: Why you trying to serve if you only a shorty?

Shorty: I'm thirteen!

The Bus

LeAlan: How dare you sell that! When you sell them ready rocks to that hype, you ain't getting the ends—it's the man with the master plan who be racking up the money! Someday he'll put a bullet in your head!

Shorty: No, I carry a nine.

LeAlan: You carry a nine?

Shorty: Hell yeah!

[We get on the bus . . .]

Bus Driver: Pay your bus fare, sir.

Lloyd: I'm only six years old.

Bus Driver: Pay your bus fare, sir. I see you out here every day. You ride the bus every day!

[We pay our fare. Shorty only has a transfer.]

Bus Driver: You can't ride with that transfer, sir!

LeAlan: If you serving, you got money, don't you? Man, you supposed to be serving and you ain't got no ends? Oooh, man.

[Shorty can't get on the bus.]

Lloyd: Can't even afford bus fare!

LeAlan: Can't even afford bus fare! And he's talking about serving ready rocks. I should have just smacked him soon as he said that! He looked like he needed to be in the mental health clinic.

Lloyd: Talked like it too!

•   •   •

We take bus rides whenever Lloyd wins some ends, or if either one of us gets some money or we just get bored. Got a dollar—get a transfer and just ride to the end of the line. Sometimes we act the fool on the bus and attract attention. Mostly we just talk about anything that pops up in our mind.

LeAlan: Man, I'm tired!

Lloyd: No school tomorrow!

LeAlan: Thank God. If it was school tomorrow I wouldn't go. Five days a week is enough! I don't see how them Chinese people go to school seven days out of the week.

Lloyd: No days off?

LeAlan: No days! They go to school the whole year round.

Lloyd: What about the holidays?

LeAlan: No holidays.

Lloyd: Summer vacation?

LeAlan: Nope. That's why they're smarter than us. They're the majority of the world—there's a couple billion Oriental people.

Lloyd: Oriental—don't you spell like O-r-i-e-n-t-a-l?

LeAlan: I don't know. I can spell on paper good, I just can't spell in my mind. O-r-i-e-n-t-a-l. I think that's right.

Lloyd: 'Cause that's the name on the ramen noodles. Don't you know those noodles that you eat?

LeAlan: Yeah, I know them. Oriental noodles. When I be hungry I get some chicken ones. Chicken ramen noodles.

Lloyd: You put eggs in yours?

LeAlan: My sister does—she puts hot dogs in and everything. I be looking at her when she do it—they look like brains, man!

Lloyd: I don't think I could talk now. I'm tired. I think I'm about to have a hernia.

LeAlan: This lady's pushing this bus! She putting the pedal to the metal. [The driver hits the brakes.]

LeAlan: Whew! We almost hit a car! We almost hit it. I think we did. . . . No, we didn't. I was scared there for a minute—I almost had a heart attack.

Lloyd: We almost could have died on this bus. We was just about to have a accident. Lucky we ain't get hit. If we would have had an accident, you think we would be hurt?

LeAlan: I would have faked it—I would have sued: *"My neck hurts, I can't move!"* I would have sued for a million dollars! *"My nose broke!"*

Lloyd: You would have been crying if your nose broke!

LeAlan: *"Aw, my nose—I hurt my nose!"*

Lloyd: Would rather have a rubber nose or a plastic nose? I ain't talking about the kind like Michael Jackson. . . .

LeAlan: A rubber nose. 'Cause if I have a fight and they hit me it'd just bounce right off and repel back at them and hit them in the face.

Lloyd: I'm so hungry I don't know what to do. Feel like the old man that lived in the shoe.

LeAlan: Rinky dinky dog . . . What's your favorite food? Breakfast food, lunch food, or dinner?

Lloyd: Can't say. . . . Let me see . . . Dinner food. Look at that sign: ABORTION EQUALS MURDER.

LeAlan: ABORTION EQUALS MURDER. That's the hippies who write that. If a girl wants to have an abortion, she got the right to an abortion. But she ain't gonna abort my child, 'cause I'm gonna have a million shorties.

Lloyd: How you gonna take care of a million shorties?

LeAlan: Bread and water.

Lloyd: If everyone gets two dollars, you gonna get about two million dollars for your aid checks!

LeAlan: I have a headache!

Lloyd: You had a headache for two weeks. I like to have blisters. I like to look at them. When you get a blister, do you wait till it busts?

LeAlan: I bust it.

Lloyd: Takes too long if you gotta wait till it busts.

LeAlan: Just chilling out today. Ain't nothing else to do. Lloyd won some ends, and we just rode to the end of the line. It's 3:54, forty-six degrees, and we're taking you on a tour of our lives!

CHAPTER 8

PEACE OUT: 1993

Hello. This is LeAlan again with my final and last diary. Me and my friend Lloyd Newman just did a description of our life for a week, and we want to give you kids in America a message: Don't look at ghetto kids as different. You might not want to invite us to your parties, you might think we'll rob you blind when you got your back turned. But don't look at us like that. Don't look at us like we're an alien or an android or an animal or something. We have a hard life, but we're sensitive. Ghetto kids are not a different breed —we're human.

Some people might say, "That boy don't know what he's talkin' about!" But I know what I'm talking about. I'm dealing from the heart because I've been dealing with this for thirteen years. These are my final words, but you'll be hearing from me again, 'cause I'm an up-and-rising activist. Peace out.

PART II

DEATH—1995

LeAlan (left) and Lloyd

CHAPTER 9

MESSENGERS

On October 13, 1994, a little boy was murdered in the Ida B. Wells. Five-year-old Eric Morse was thrown out of a fourteenth-story window by two other little boys, supposedly because he wouldn't steal candy for them. The story was big news all across America.

For a couple of weeks, there were reporters and politicians all over Ida B. Wells. Jesse Jackson had a press conference. President Clinton talked about the incident in a speech and so did Newt Gingrich. Everybody jumped on the bandwagon and said, "We're gonna change things in the Ida B. Wells!" "We're gonna do something about these buildings!" "We're gonna do this" and "We're gonna do that." But after a little while everyone left, and nothing changed. Not surprising—when it comes to the Ida B. Wells, politicians keep sweeping the dirt under the rug and it just keeps piling up. The problems get bigger and bigger every day, every minute, and every second.

So in January 1995, when we were both fifteen years old, Lloyd and I decided to try to do something: to be messengers to the world about the Ida B. Wells, and let them know that something has got to change. We picked up our microphones again to find out the story of Eric Morse.

3833 South Langley

CHAPTER 10

THE SCENE OF THE CRIME

Everybody in the 'hood heard the same story about how Eric Morse was murdered. The incident involved four kids—two victims: five-year-old Eric Morse and his eight-year-old brother, Derrick; and two assailants: a ten-year-old named Johnny and an eleven-year-old named Tyrone. Supposedly, Johnny and Tyrone tried to get Eric to steal candy for them from Jewel Supermarket (that's where all the shorties in The Wells steal from). Eric told his mother, Toni Morse, and she went and told Tyrone's mother. Tyrone got in trouble. Johnny and Tyrone decided to seek revenge on Eric and his brother.

On Thursday, October 13, Johnny and Tyrone saw Eric Morse and his older brother, Derrick, outside of one of the high-rises in the Ida Bees. Johnny and Tyrone asked Eric and Derrick to come upstairs to look at their clubhouse—a vacant apartment on the fourteenth floor. The four shorties went upstairs and pulled off the boards covering the door to apartment 1405. When they got inside, Johnny and Tyrone grabbed Eric and held him out of a window. Eight-year-old Derrick grabbed his brother and pulled him back in. Then Johnny and Tyrone took Eric to a second window and held him out. Derrick grabbed Eric again, but this time Tyrone bit Derrick's hand and he had to let go. Eric fell fourteen stories. Derrick ran down fourteen flights of stairs to try to save his brother—he thought he could catch him before he hit the ground. Eric was pronounced dead ten minutes later.

• • •

The Fourteenth Floor

The killing of Eric Morse happened at 3833 South Langley—a building exactly halfway between our two houses. I can see the spot from
my back porch and Lloyd can see it from his front porch. Number
3833 is one of four high-rise buildings in The Wells (most of The
Wells buildings are low-rise, like Lloyd's house). The high-rises are
called the Darrow Homes, but we call them the Def Homes. One of
the buildings is just abandoned, and the rest are mostly empty. It's the
worst part of The Wells to live in.

●   ●   ●

Going in the building now. Don't need keys and don't need to sign
in—just walk right through—they don't ask questions. Two elevators—
one for odd floors, one for even floors. Usually don't work, so you got
to use the stairs. . . .

I'm walking on the fourteenth floor now. Caged-in hallway. It's
freezing and it's not even winter. Only three or four people live on this
floor—about ten vacant apartments. Another boarded-up apartment,
another vacant apartment. I can count on my hands and toes how
many people live in this building. . . .

On the thirteenth floor now. Oh, I hate that smell—this puddle of
piss has been here since I was born! What's this, a dead cat? Nope—
alive. The cat's just trying to stay warm. He's got nine lives—looks like
he used up about three. Little orange crates in the hallway that shorties play basketball on. Pampers and dookie.

More vacant apartments. Here's an apartment where someone
lives, but they've boarded up their windows. A lot of people do that:
someone breaks into your apartment or little kids throw rocks and
break your glass, so just to be on the safe side you board yourselves in
and live in darkness. No windows. The only light is from your lightbulb. They've been doing that for years.

I would not live in here—no way, nohow! You could put me to
death before I live in something like this! And 3833 is the best one out
of all of them in the Def Homes. 3833. I hate walking through here,
man.

●   ●   ●

Lloyd and I spent a lot of time in 3833 trying to find out what we
could about life in the building and the death of Eric Morse.

The building seems like it's mostly vacant, especially the top floors.
Most of the people didn't want to talk to us anyway—I guess they

Living in Darkness

feared that someone might think they said the wrong thing and take revenge.

LeAlan: Anybody home? Anybody home? Ghost town.

Lloyd: Man, Shorty fell from way up here!

LeAlan: Way up here!

Lloyd: I know Shorty was scared when he was falling. He was wondering, "Will I die?"

LeAlan: But he was so young he wouldn't know if he wanted to live or wanted to die.

Lloyd: Nobody wants to die. Even a baby—you can tell from when they cry. When you cry that means you don't want to die.

LeAlan: I wonder how he felt falling from fourteen stories? What the hell would go through your mind?

Lloyd: I'd be thinking about how I'm going to land and if I'm going to survive. I'd be thinking about how it is in heaven. But I know I won't have that much time to think.

LeAlan: How long do you think it took for him to drop? Maybe four or five seconds?

Lloyd: Every second he was going faster and faster. . . .

LeAlan: Man, I don't know what I'd be thinking about. I probably just would have said a prayer or something.

Lloyd: That's all you could have said.

LeAlan: "God forgive me for my sins. Amen. . . ." Hey, Lloyd, since Shorty was so young, you know he went to heaven. . . .

Lloyd: Yeah.

LeAlan: You think they got a playground in heaven for those shorties?

Lloyd: Nope. They don't got a playground in heaven for nobody.

LeAlan: How you figure there ain't a playground for little kids?

Lloyd: There ain't. God didn't make it special for nobody!

LeAlan: But what's Shorty gonna do up there? He wasn't old enough to do anything bad enough to go to hell. So what could he do up there?

Lloyd: I got to think. . . .

LeAlan: Shorty was nothing but five. So what's he gonna do up there—chill with the grown-ups? Or is he reincarnated? Maybe he's a little bird or something. . . .

•   •   •

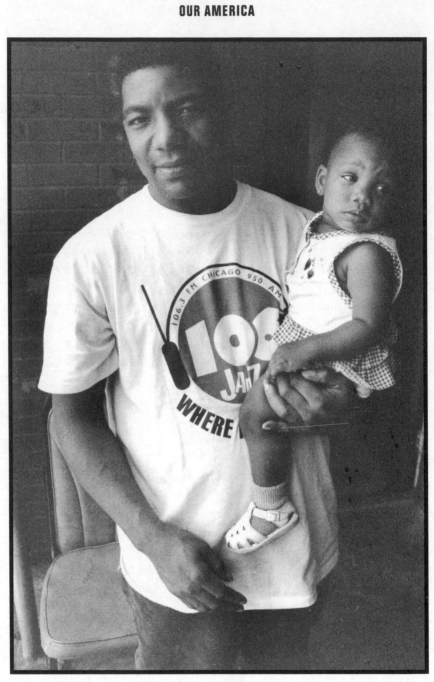

William and Cashai Sewell

The fourteenth floor wasn't totally abandoned. One day we found William Sewell, who lives in an apartment at the end of the hallway. He told us he was 33 years old and had three kids.

Sewell: When I was growing up it was different. I grew up in the projects, but where we lived at we had open fields and spaces. It wasn't a lot of gangs and guns and drugs then, so it was better for kids. We had a chance to play. Now my kids don't have a chance to play. I don't let them go out. I got to keep them in the house, and that's detrimental for young people. The kids in this building deserve a chance: not being around drugs, being able to go to different places and see different things in life. Because life is fruitful and they should be able to go grab some of the meat of life. You boys get away from this environment at times, right? You get out and you see different things? Well, that's the way it has to be. Kids that grow up in this environment and don't see other things and don't know of light beyond this tunnel of darkness—they don't grow and they get stuck in this type of mentality.

· · ·

LeAlan: Hey, Lloyd, what do you think happened to Eric?

Lloyd: I think that those boys thought that since Eric told on them they weren't going to be able to steal candy anymore. So they figured that if they threw him out of the window, they could just go right back to stealing stuff again.

LeAlan: Right. They went off their first reactions and didn't think it through. Their first reaction was to throw him off the fourteenth floor. If they went to their second or third reaction we wouldn't be doing this story.

Lloyd: I didn't even know it happened until about four hours later. I ran over to the building and there was no one over there—just white tape and reporters—so I went back in the house. It didn't matter to me.

LeAlan: When I first heard, I was in my room listening to tapes and my momma said someone just got thrown out the window. I had five minutes of sympathy, then I was like "Man, it happens. Life goes on." I'm long past the phase of "They're dead, I'm never going to see them again!" I got past that stage a long time ago. . . .

Lloyd: It's just so bad around here that it can't surprise you.

LeAlan: Death ain't nothing new around here. . . .

Annie Smith

Lloyd: Everyone's born to die. You do what you have to do to live, but in the long run you're gonna die regardless.

LeAlan: Here today, gone tomorrow. . . .

Lloyd: You just got to try to take care of yourself any way you can until the day comes that you have to go.

LeAlan: If you took the time to think about all the death that goes on around here, you'd go crazy! But that shows you how life is valued now when ten-year-old kids kill for a piece of candy. Life has the value of a quarter now—not even that! It's funny, if you think about it, but it's sad. I mean, killing over a piece of candy?

Lloyd: They were raised like that, I guess. They were just following footsteps. That's how it all begins.

LeAlan: No one around them appreciates life, so why should they? Look at the building—you walk in and it smells like urine, you walk up the stairs and it's dark, broken lights. When you live in filth, your mind takes in filth and you feel nothing.

•   •   •

On the thirteenth floor we found Annie Smith, who lives in the apartment directly beneath the one Eric Morse was thrown from.

Annie Smith: Before that night I used to hear noise upstairs all the time and report to housing that people were up there—vandalizing it, knocking holes in the wall, and things like that. I used to go upstairs and say, "You guys got to stop making noise up here!" It happened so much that after a while I could just open my door and they would leave. It was kind of like a game after that, and I figured maybe they'd slow down a bit.

It was very quiet the night that it happened. I was in the back room with my children—my fifteen-year-old boy, my nine-year-old son, my two daughters—we were back there watching TV. See, my children stay in. They *do not* go outside—we have activities in our house that keep them occupied. So we were watching *The Godfather* on tape, and all I heard was a chair scooting back. I said to my kids, "Oh, it's so quiet up there tonight. No one's making any noise!"

About an hour later, after it got dark, my daughter came in and said, "Mother! Mother! A little boy just fell out the window!" Just like that. I looked outside and there were police and everything downstairs. Someone had dropped the little boy from the window. And it

Shorties in 3833

was kind of strange because I almost felt responsible, because had I gone upstairs when I heard the chair go back, maybe I could have stopped something. But then I can't hold myself responsible for somebody's parents who should have been looking out for their child at that time of night. I couldn't hold myself responsible for their actions.

It's sad that it happened to Eric Morse, but it's attention we had to have. We had to have national attention because this building is in a crisis and we *do* need help. Sometimes bad things are meant to happen so it can bring attention to the worse things that will happen if someone doesn't pay attention.

Where Eric Fell

CHAPTER 11

FROM THE OUTSIDE, LOOKING IN

These are the dudes that hang out around the corner from my house. I walk by them every time I go to 3833:

Dude #1: You rapping today?

LeAlan: No, man, I don't rap. I'm talking about the little guy that got threw out the window. Doing a story about him.

Dude #2: You a young reporter?

LeAlan: Yeah . . .

Dude #2: What's your name, man?

LeAlan: LeAlan.

Dude #2: LeAlan? You got a professional name too!

LeAlan: Yeah, I'm doing a story about that little guy Eric Morse because the media just said a whole bunch of stuff that wasn't right. I mean, this isn't the first time somebody's been thrown off one of these buildings—because gang-bangers throw each other off the roofs all the time. It's been this way for years! It just takes an incident like this to make everybody think.

Dude #2: Like years ago, remember that one time in The Wells?

LeAlan: With those ladies?

Dude #2: No, no. With the guys. One was a janitor, and one was my

101

Looking Down from the Fourteenth Floor

son's uncle. They pushed both of the guys down the elevator shaft, and they cut one guy's head off and put his thing in his mouth.

LeAlan: Yeah. It's nothing new.

Dude #2: But about that young guy? The kids who did it ain't never got a sense of feelings. They never been taught that it don't take much to kill a person. They've been looking at these cartoons, seeing people die twice on TV, and they thought that this little boy couldn't die.

Dude #3: It ain't like Bugs Bunny—go down and splash, next scene he's up running around getting chased again.

Dude #2: A child can't have a sense to push somebody out a window! Throw a boy out the window just for candy? If he killed for candy, imagine what he would do for twenty or thirty dollars—he'd shoot the President!

Dude #1: If they killed for candy, they be ready to take out the whole neighborhood just to get a rep, you know?

LeAlan: Young soldiers, man. That's all they are. Young mercenaries.

Dude #3: We talk about it so much but it seems like nothing don't ever get done. We could sit here and talk all day, but what's getting done?

Dude #1: I like what you're doing, brother, I like what you're doing.

Dude #2: Think of the good ideas, man, that you can to tell to the people. . . .

Dude #3: Anything that can make a change would help. Anything that can make a change would help.

Dude #2: Hey, man, I better go. . . .

LeAlan: All right, man. Stay up.

Dude #2: Stay up, brother.

•　　　•　　　•

LeAlan: We're standing right here where the little dude got killed. How's that make you feel? That's like walking over a graveyard, ain't it?

Lloyd: LeAlan, why does it make you feel different standing right here? You ain't standing on his grave or nothing, you're just standing on grass. It happened right here, but it ain't right here.

LeAlan: That's like Indian burial ground, homie—you ain't gonna catch no Indian walking on another Indian's grave or where he died. It's just a feeling, man. You never know—Shorty's soul could be looking down at us now, doing a story about him.

103

The Apartment Eric Was Dropped From

•   •   •

In February 1995, we met Vince Lane outside 3833. At the time, Lane was the chairman of the Chicago Housing Authority (CHA), the agency in charge of all public housing in the city.

LeAlan: *We're now standing at the site where Eric Morse was thrown from a fourteenth-story window. To a young person living in this community, it looks like a fourteen-story cemetery. If you lived in this community and you were a young person, what would be your thought?*
Lane: My thought would be it would be hell.

Lloyd: *Would you want your kids growing up in these public houses?*
Absolutely not. I don't want my kids growing up here. I don't want *any* kid growing up here the way it is today. Because there's no way a kid can grow up in an environment where ninety-three percent of the families are on some form of government assistance. No supervised playgrounds, no activities. You don't have any of the things that kids should have in order to be children and grow up to be healthy adults. This is no environment for a kid.

LeAlan: *Now we're on the fourteenth floor. This is not a penthouse view. In the distance you can see the Stateway Apartments. If you look more to the left you can see the Robert Taylor Homes. You see two or three liquor stores. . . .*
And the other part of this view is you see young people on the street who basically have nowhere to go. They're there now, and three hours from now they'll be there. And that's the difference between a healthy community and public housing. People in healthy communities have things to do—*positive* things to do. People in public housing have nothing to do. Right here young people are trapped. You stand up here on the fourteenth floor and you look around, and people are trapped within the boundaries of this development.

LeAlan: *We're now at the door of the vacant apartment where Eric Morse was thrown off the building. Chairman Lane, what kind of problems do vacant apartments pose on crime in the CHA?*
Vacant apartments are like a cancer, and the bad guys know that they are like cancers. They get into the vacant apartments and they gradu-

ally eat away at the fabric of a building. They intimidate the decent people who are on either side of a vacant unit until pretty soon they get driven away, and then the gang-bangers take over another unit and another unit, and before you know it you've got buildings that are seventy percent vacant. And sometimes it's not even a gang-banger in the vacant apartments—you get kids who use the vacant apartments as their clubhouse, like kids in the suburbs would use a tree house.

LeAlan: *Chairman Lane, how did this problem get to what it is now?*
I think we have to look at the genesis of these developments. I was around Chicago when they built the high-rises. And before they built them these were nice low-rise, low-density neighborhoods—single-story, two-flat buildings where everybody knew everybody. When they built the expressways and had urban renewal, they destroyed a lot of that housing and built these high-rise buildings. And they built them cheaply. So there was cost in mind: "Why should you spend money on poor people?" And there was also an element of racism: the containment of blacks. When you look at the concentration of public housing in Chicago there's nothing like it anywhere else in America.

We've got to get back to the point where we don't stack poor people on top of each other. Also, there are no role models: fathers, brothers, sisters that get up and go to work every day and who are doing positive things. We don't have Boy Scouts, Cub Scouts, Little League—almost anything. So when you don't have any alternatives, I don't know why society would be surprised at what happens in public housing today.

CHAPTER 12

A BREAKTHROUGH

We went back into 3833 over and over again, but had a hard time finding out anything about the crime. The lower we went in the building, the less people would open their doors for us—a lot of them said they never even *heard* of Eric Morse. It was frustrating! But one day, working on the ninth floor, we knocked on a door covered by graffiti. A little boy answered. He said his name was Isaac.

LeAlan: How old are you, sir?

Isaac: Thirty-seven.

LeAlan: You're thirty-seven years old, and you're standing about four feet eleven. How old are you for real, sir?

Isaac: Eleven.

LeAlan: How long have you been living here?

Isaac: Six years.

LeAlan: Did you know Eric Morse?

Isaac: Yeah.

LeAlan: Was he a close friend of yours?

Isaac: You could say.

LeAlan: Did you know the people that did it?

Isaac: Yes. The boy who killed him was in my classroom.

LeAlan: What type of kids were they? Were they very bad?

Isaac: Yes. 'Cause when they used to do bad stuff, I used to go. Like sometimes we used to go downtown and steal gold chains. But

Isaac

when Eric got killed, I got scared. I said I wasn't going to be with them no more.

LeAlan: Why did you want to run with that crowd?

Isaac: 'Cause when you don't have nothing else to do and you see somebody else doing something, then you want to get down with them.

While we talked, Isaac held a little baby in his arms. The infant belonged to his sister, Tymeka. She also came out to talk to us. Tymeka is our age, and I recognized her from the eighth grade when we used to compete in the Academic Olympics. Tymeka told us that she was close to Johnny, the ten-year-old boy involved in the murder. Of the two boys, Johnny was supposed to be the *really* bad one—a menace that ran wild through the streets of the Ida B. Wells. But Tymeka says she knew a different Johnny.

Tymeka: Johnny was my baby. Everybody used to label him as "that little bad sucker!" But I got close to Johnny and he became like a little brother to me.

At first when I'd see him I'd say, "What's up, bad boy?" And he wouldn't answer me 'cause he was quiet and didn't reveal himself to too many people. So I'd say, "Why you dissing me like that?" And I kept talking to him like a regular person. So after a while I became a friend. When he'd see me he'd say, "Hey, Tymeka, what's up?" And I believe that what happened was a freak accident, an honest mistake.

I know this from experience, O.K.? I have a little brother and a little sister that are twins. When they used to really get on my nerves, I used to say, "I'm gonna throw your butt out this window!" And I'd hold them out the window—just to scare them. So I feel that's what happened to Eric—they wanted to scare him so that the next time he would get that candy for them, and they just dropped him by accident. And I believe truly in my heart that's how it happened. That baby slipped out the window. They didn't throw that baby out the window. Who's that cruel? An adult would do something like that, but not no children.

Johnny and Tyrone were normal little bad kids, just like me. I myself stole from Jewel. I fought and went to the police station. Their background is like that—they didn't have a background of torturing

Tymeka and Deandre

little babies. Johnny was in trouble with the law because he didn't have the right guidance to scold him and tell him, "No is no!" "Right is right!" "Wrong is wrong!" His father was incarcerated. He had a drug-abusive mother—who probably wasn't raised right by her mother either—and the drugs were taking over her life. She loved her children, but she didn't have control over them. They would curse at her. I'd hear Johnny tell her, "Shut up!" And I'd tell him, "You don't talk to your mother like that!" He understood me, and when I was in his presence he did not act like that.

I have a little cousin, Dovontae. He can be real evil and stubborn. Back when my great-grandmother passed we were all at my grandmother's house, trying to clean it up so she could come home to a house of happiness. We said to the kids, "Help clean up!" So Dovontae says, "I ain't doing nothing! Don't tell me what to do! You ain't my momma!" And the more we demand, the stubborner he gets and the more he refuses to do what we say. So I grabbed my cousin and I put my arms around him and told him, "Come on, don't make a scene like this." And I cried. And then he just grabbed me back, and hugged me and let out tears. He cooperated after that, you know? So you can get beside a person. The person you think is the dirtiest, meanest person in the world got a side you can get to—if you know how to do it.

Johnny and Tyrone need to suffer the consequences to show them the difference between what to do and what not to do. But they also need help. They need counseling, and they need therapy. I know they will never forget what they did to that child. It will always be a dark space in their head—every day, every minute, every hour. I just pray to God. I pray for all them children.

While we're leaving, Tymeka's brother Isaac was staring out the window.

LeAlan: When you look out your window, what do you see?
Isaac: Everything.
LeAlan: You see good things?
Isaac: Sometimes. Like when nobody's out there selling drugs. That's a good thing. Or if I don't see nobody getting beat up or nothing.
LeAlan: What's a bad thing you see when you look out the window?
Isaac: People getting beat up, shot down. Just people going crazy.
[Tymeka's baby starts crying.]

LeAlan: Is that a boy or a girl?

Isaac: Boy.

LeAlan: Do you want that boy to grow up just like you?

Isaac: Nope. I'd make him be a better person than me.

LeAlan: Like how? Making sure his friends don't die like that?

Isaac: Yeah, him too. Not just his friends. Him too.

LeAlan: O.K., Isaac, you stay strong.

Lloyd: Bye, Isaac.

[We leave the apartment.]

LeAlan: That shows you how lonely these kids are. . . .

Lloyd: Why, 'cause they want to talk?

LeAlan: They're just like M&Ms—all hard on the outside and sweet on the inside.

Lloyd: You saw how he was about to cry?

LeAlan: Yeah, I saw that. . . .

Lloyd: He was about to shed those tears, boy. His eyes got *real* watery. . . . If you had a dollar or something you would have gave it to him, huh?

LeAlan: Yeah. He was a nice young man.

CHAPTER 13

JUVENILE JUSTICE

In February 1995, almost a year before the trial of Johnny and Tyrone, we went to the Juvenile Court building in downtown Chicago to find out more about the Eric Morse case. Our first interview was with Kay Hanlon, the supervising prosecutor.

LeAlan: *What went through your mind when you first heard about this crime?*
Kay Hanlon: Well, I've been in Juvenile Court for almost two years and I've seen some pretty horrible things, and the first thing I could think about was that this is probably one of the most horrible things I've seen.

LeAlan: *Is this a typical everyday case for you?*
It seems that lately there's been more violent crimes committed by kids. So this is a pretty typical case, except they were a little bit young—most of the murders that I see are thirteen- or fourteen-year-olds killing each other with guns. Ten and eleven is pretty young.

LeAlan: *When did you first see younger offenders doing bigger crimes?*
I would say probably within the last six to eight months I've seen a real increase in the brutality of the crimes, and also younger kids doing the real brutal stuff.

Kay Hanlon

LeAlan: *Do you have any sympathy toward the young men that did this or toward the young people that live in the buildings? Can you relate to them?*

I certainly have sympathy toward the young kids who live in the buildings, because this kind of violence is hard for an *adult* to deal with, so I imagine it's a lot harder for a kid to deal with. The eight-year-old brother? I have a ton of sympathy for him having to watch his five-year-old brother get thrown out of a window—I think that's going to affect him for the rest of his life. And yes, certainly anybody else who lives there who may have walked by and seen the child, or who just even heard about it and has to walk by there every day and see where it happened—I feel sorry for everyone. But I can't even begin to imagine what went through a ten- and eleven-year-old's mind to throw a five-year-old out a window.

LeAlan: *Do you think this could have been a mistake?*
No.

LeAlan: *Or an accident of some sort?*
No, I don't think so. Actually I'm sure that it couldn't be an accident because of the way that it happened. It was premeditated, it was planned, it was thought out. And it didn't only happen once, it happened twice: first his eight-year-old brother was able to save him and pull him back in. Then he was held out the window again, and as his eight-year-old brother was holding on to him, one of the kids bit his hand so that he had to let go. And that is definitely premeditated first-degree murder as far as I'm concerned.

LeAlan: *Do you think society had anything to do with affecting their minds to throw a five-year-old out that window?*
No, I don't. And probably because I really believe in responsibility for your actions. I tend to think that even though you're ten or eleven, you know right from wrong. You've been through a little bit in life. You know what death is, hopefully. You know that when you throw somebody out a fourteenth-floor window they're going to die. So I really don't blame society. These kids knew right from wrong.

(Left to right) Dave McMahon, Rick Hutt, Peter Parry, Dave Hirschboeck

LeAlan: *Do you feel that these children were bred in a life of violence? Because I live in that community, and it seems to be getting worse and worse and worse every year.*

I certainly think that their background is different than a lot of other kids. I mean, anybody who commits this kind of crime probably has gone through something in their lives. But then again I look at other kids. For example, you grew up in that community, and look what you're doing. It's a far cry from committing a first-degree murder.

•   •   •

After we met Kay Hanlon, we went up one floor in the Juvenile Court building to talk to the four attorneys from the Juvenile Public Defender's office representing Johnny, the ten-year-old defendant.

LeAlan: *What were your first thoughts when you heard about this crime?*

Dave Hirschboeck: Well, my first thoughts were that it's a tragedy all around. When I heard the defendants were ten and eleven years old, I was very sad, and when I heard the age of Mr. Morse I was also very sad. It's a sad situation in every respect.

Peter Parry: This case occurred in an area where a lot of my cases come from. I've known our client before and I know the area, and it's just another tragedy in that part of the city.

LeAlan: *When did you first start seeing more and more young people coming into the courts?*

Parry: Well, I've been a public defender here for a little under four years, and in just four years I've seen the type of violence increase and the amount of violence increase. These types of alleged crimes did not really occur four years ago. But all of us in this room have had many murder cases assigned to us in the last several months. I've had five at one time. I know the others have had many cases too.

Rick Hutt: Rather than how long it's been going on, I focus on the kind of violence I see. It makes less and less sense. I can kind of understand it if somebody's mad at somebody or wants revenge. I don't like it, but I can understand the motivation. But now the motivations behind these things are getting less and less easy to understand. I'm seeing people pulling out guns over the smallest things and shooting—and not even shooting at somebody, just shooting in a general direction. I'm seeing little kids getting killed. I had to defend some-body where the victim was eighteen months old. I've seen violence ever since I got here. Now I'm just seeing it get more and more sense-less.

LeAlan: *Do you feel that the young people that did this crime got used to so much violence that it was nothing for them to do?*
Hirschboeck: These people that we represent are exposed to violence. They see shootings, they see stabbings, they see *everything*. They see things that *I've* never seen! Does that affect these children and is that what's going on? I think that's a big part of what's going on.

LeAlan: *This is something that I said many years ago: These young kids have a mind state very similar to a Vietnam veteran, because when I walk out of my front door I could get shot just like a Vietnam veteran could walk in the bush and get shot by a guerrilla.*
Hirschboeck: What you're saying is very apropos to what's going on here. You talk about Vietnam, and there was this whole history of post-traumatic stress syndrome, and I think that's what we're seeing now. Especially with kids this young. When our government sent people to Vietnam, the violence they were exposed to affected them psychologically—and those were people that were *sent* there to kill and fight. Now think about you boys, and these boys that are charged with this crime.

LeAlan: *When we were knocking on the doors of the apartment building where it happened—I mean, this touched me—a young man that answered the door said he was thirty-seven years old. We ended up stay-ing a half hour to interview him, and the little guy almost came to tears. I know I'm a strong person, but I look at that and say, "Life is shit!" I hate to be that frank around all you adults.*
Dave McMahon: No, not at all. And I think there are kids your age . . .
Hirschboeck: Who've given up on life.
Hutt: But, you know, the thing that I've noticed—in all the time I've been here I've never once seen a kid who isn't a little boy. We get kids up to seventeen years old, and I've seen a kid sixteen years eight months, six foot one, been gang-banging for five years, carries a gun, his father's incarcerated, his mother hasn't seen him in months—and

I've talked to that kid and within five minutes (not because I'm a great person, but just if you take the time) within *five minutes* I see a little boy. And you have little boys over there who have never had a chance to be little boys. They never got a chance to go run around a lake, they never got a chance to play ball, they never got a chance to do all the things that we did, and I guess you're doing in a way, and I don't care what they're accused of doing or how big and how mean that they want to be, five minutes tops you start talking to little boys. They can all be reached. Every one of them—they're all savable. Every one of them!

Suggs Miller

CHAPTER 14

FALLING THROUGH THE CRACKS

Having a family can sometimes be a big help when you're working on a story. One afternoon my cousin Scootchie took me to meet his friend Suggs Miller, who is president of the Local School Council at Doolittle West. Both Johnny and Tyrone went to Doolittle West (which goes from kindergarten to fourth grade) before going on to Doolittle East (which goes from fifth to eighth grade), where they were in school at the time of the incident. Suggs came over to my house for an interview.

Suggs: I knew both Tyrone and Johnny, but I had a lot more to do with the younger boy, Johnny. I can remember that when he started in kindergarten, Johnny came to school with two bags of rock cocaine. Kindergarten. He gave one to his friend, and he kept one. The friend swallowed his, Johnny stuck his in his pants once the teacher saw them. And these kids were five or six years old at the time, you know? They'd have to have seen something to know either to swallow it or to stick it down their pants. Where did they get it from? Had to be in his household.

Johnny's mom, unfortunately, was one of the people that got hooked on something that was uncontrollable. She would always say that she couldn't do anything with him, but it's hard to do anything with a child when they see these types of things going on. Expecting the kids to grow up themselves doesn't do it. You can't tell them: "This is right and that's wrong," when they constantly see you doing wrong. And basically he had nowhere to live because Mom had got evicted from her apartment, so they were squatting in 3833—four of them in one bedroom. And it's rough when you really feel that you don't have anywhere to go. So that's how that is.

But when Johnny was in school, I could talk to him. He was very sensitive—he'd flare up and fight in a minute—but I could talk to him and he would calm down and talk to me. And it just seemed all he needed was someone to spend some time with him. So when it happened, it made me feel bad because I felt like I should've spent more time with him. We had tried at Doolittle to get some help for Johnny—we tested him, we put him in a Special Ed class, but he needed more than that, and unfortunately we weren't able to get it to him in time.

Tyrone's little brother is still at the school. It's been very emotional for him. He gets upset every time the kids mention it. After it happened I had to see him home a couple of times because he thought the kids were going to jump on him because of what his brother did. Johnny's brother—we ended up transferring him from Doolittle because of the way kids are—kids can be very cruel!

Eric's brother was at the school too. It was very emotional for Derrick. I'm talking *very* emotional. The statement was made: "Oh, you let him go!" And it made him feel like he killed his brother. But on the day of his brother's funeral we had a plaque for him at Doolittle and told him that he was a hero because he hung in there with his brother to the very end. He grabbed his brother *twice* before he was bitten to make him let his brother go. The day of the funeral he still had some scars. For a young man his age that was very strong and very courageous—because they could have grabbed him and hung him out the window too. And he didn't run off and leave his brother. Downstairs they told him to go get his mother, and he told them that he wasn't going to leave—he had to wait there until his brother woke up. It was just . . . It was heavy.

•   •   •

Dr. Teddy Osentowski was Johnny's Special Ed teacher at Doolittle East for the one month of school before the incident occurred.

Lloyd: *What was Johnny like?*
Dr. Osentowski: I have to give you a little anecdotal thing. The first day he came into the classroom I wanted them to sit in assigned seats so that I could get to know names. And, of course, he refused to sit in the seat that I had assigned to him and he went to the back of the room and sat. Well, I'm not a teacher who says, "O.K.," so I went back and told him he'd have to move up to the front. He tried to hit me, so I grabbed his arm and held on to it. When he saw that I wasn't going to let go and I wasn't gonna change my mind, then of course he did go up to the seat where he should have been.

LeAlan:*What are some of the things that you think made him a hostile indiviual toward you, toward the school system, and toward life?*
The schools failed Johnny. They had not met his needs. When he came to me he had not learned to read, and yet he was ten years old. So I was just another person in the system that he had to encounter. But after I had been with him for a while, he was one of the most docile and nicest-acting persons that I have ever had any encounter with. And he tried to do his work. The child was actually *trying* to do this work. So he was fitting in just fine as far as I was concerned. And it was a total surprise to me when I heard about the incident.

Lloyd: *How did you feel that morning when you heard about the crime?*
I heard about it the night before, but I did not know it was Johnny. When I went into the school that morning some teachers were clustered around the office, and they were talking about this "bad boy" and what he had done, how they knew he was going to get into trouble and it served him right and so forth and so on. And I still didn't know who they were talking about. So I walked over to the group of teachers and I asked, "What are you guys talking about?" And they said, "What happened last night." And I said, "Who was the child?" And when they said it was Johnny—well, that was *my* child. And I felt very hurt, because I think he and I had an understanding. And I really felt that he and I were going to go places, because we had been able to interact up until the night of the incident.

And it was very tough for the class. The children, you know, become somewhat cynical when things like this happen because of where they

123

Dr. Teddy Osentowski

live and how they have to live. So they came in as though they were talking about "Somebody stole my mother's purse last night." You know, it's just another notch on the road of knowing where you are. And we did not receive a crisis team until almost the end of the second week, so nobody was there to help the students. I talked a little bit about it, but I don't qualify as a counselor. And when the so-called experts came, they didn't stay long—I think they were there about forty-five minutes, if that long. I had twelve to fifteen kids in that class, and they needed more than that.

LeAlan: *What are some of the things you think could have stopped that incident from happening?*
You know, I've thought about that, and at the moment I don't think anything. The reason I'm saying that is that I don't think that Johnny had been taught to deal with his feelings. He was impulsive. I was not there, so I don't know, but if indeed he did the actual pushing, it was, as far as I'm concerned, a very impulsive thing. It was based on him not knowing and not being taught how to deal with his feelings.

Lloyd: *What do you think of Johnny passing with the bad grades that he had?*
How could you let a kid stay in school that many years—grades one through five—and he can't read? No one taught him to read! Had I been able to hold him longer, I could have taught him. He would have opened up more, because at some time all kids open up. Johnny was not the first Johnny I've had. The school system is full of Johnnys. That *same school* is full of Johnnys. And I don't know if it fooled other people, but I think Johnny was just putting on a facade, a front. Tough guy.

LeAlan: *Why do you think he had to have that tough guy image?*
To survive. To survive.

Tommy Jenkins. (He didn't want his face photographed.)

CHAPTER 15

BOTH SIDES
OF THE LAW

In April 1995, we drove to the Hill Correctional Center in Galesburg, Illinois (about three hours from Chicago), to meet Tommy Jenkins, the father of Tyrone, the eleven-year-old involved in the crime. Tyrone was less notorious than Johnny around the 'hood. Before his father was incarcerated, Tyrone was supposedly doing O.K. in school. After Tommy went away, Tyrone started running away from home and messing up in class.

Tommy Jenkins is serving an eight-year sentence for the aggravated battery of Tyrone's mother. We interviewed him in the prison visiting room.

Lloyd: *What are some of your best memories of your son?*
Tommy Jenkins: He's warm, he's sensitive, he's understanding. He's very smart—'cause I kept him in the house. I used to work construction, and when I'd come home from work, I'd sit down and I would tutor him for three or four hours. (I probably didn't even take off my work boots!) So my son can recite the whole Civil War (which a lot of kids probably can't), and he can tell you about the Revolution. He's very intelligent for his age.

Tyrone was not bad. He was just hanging around bad company. But that's what happens to us all—you hang with the wrong people, something's eventually going to happen. And this is eventually what happened.

LeAlan: *Do you feel that your absence from seeing your son led to the alleged incident?*
Yes, it did. Because I feel that when a father and his child are separated, the child has a tendency to take the wrong route in life. Especially if the father has instilled values in his kids and has always been there for them to show them the right way and the right things to do.

It's just like if I put a pit bull in this cabinet and kept him locked away from what he wants. Soon as you open it up and let him out he's frisky, happy to be free, happy to get out. I had a dog named General Grant. Anybody in the projects will tell you he was the craziest dog over there. *Big* teeth—sometimes he used to scare me. But he loved Ty. I had to keep the dog in the closet on a big old lock and chain, and he used to be in there spinning around in circles. But I knew once I let him out he'd just run around and tear things up—excited that he's free. That's like a child: You can keep him away from the bad people and tell him, "Stay away from Shorty!" But once you're gone, that child is free to do what he wants. It's common sense.

LeAlan: *Where were you when you first heard of a little boy being thrown out the window in the community that you and your kids lived in?*
I was in Stateville Penitentiary. We was in lockdown at the time, and it came on the radio at about five o'clock in the morning. And I sat up and just felt that my baby was involved. See, when you're close to someone you get a *feeling,* and by me and my son being real tight, when I heard it over the radio I just had this premonition. So when we come off lockdown I called his mother and she was crying on the phone. But I already knew. It's just that gut feeling that you have. So me and all my buddies went to the yard, and we all bent down on our right knees and said prayers for my son and the little boy that died. There was about a hundred of us out there. A lot of people loved my son.

But I can't put a halo above Tyrone's head like he's an angel. He has to take the blame for what happened. That baby is dead. That baby is in the ground and you can't bring him back to life. They were both up there when that happened, and they both got to take the blame for what happened. I just don't want him to come out of this with that ruthless type of attitude. That's what these walls do to you—they make you hard, they make you barren, they make you cold.

I talked to him two weeks ago and he said, "Daddy, I'm getting big now." I said, "Ty, no matter what happens, I love you and I'll always be there for you." That's the type of relationship we have—Ty knows I'm going to be there for him no matter what happens. A father has an obligation to his child, a commitment. And I know that he's going to make it. A lot of people think that he ain't, but he's going to make it. He may need some time, but he's going to get through this.

●   ●   ●

Chicago Housing Authority police officers Laurie Sabatini and Donnie Hixon were partners at the Ida B. Wells from 1992 until 1994, and knew Tyrone and Johnny very well. They told us they first came across the shorties a couple of months after they started patrolling The Wells.

Laurie Sabatini: Our very first dealing with Tyrone and Johnny was when they stole a bunch of pizzas out of the grocery store. By the time we caught up with them, Johnny's mother was in the process of cooking the pizzas—which lets you know where his mother was coming from. We made them take the pizzas back. The next time was when Tyrone got caught with a bunch of heroin. He and Johnny were in a vacant apartment damaging stuff. We just happened to be on foot that day and we were going to arrest them for criminal damage to property when we discovered the heroin.

But for some reason Donnie and I took a real interest in those boys. Especially Tyrone. Johnny had a mother that was a hype, and that made it real hard to connect with him.

Donnie Hixon: But Tyrone's mother was employed. She worked at a nursing home every day trying to keep her family together, and had a motherly concern about the welfare of her children. So with us seeing that we said, "Let's try to help do something to turn this kid around."

Sabatini: Tyrone was always running away, and we would take him home in the morning, clean him up, and get him ready for school— 'cause his mom had already gone to work.

Hixon: Then we'd take him to White Castle or McDonald's, and an hour later we'd see him on the streets. . . .

Sabatini: "What the hell are you doing out here? We just took you to

Officers Laurie Sabatini and Donnie Hixon

school?" And come to find out we dropped him off and he went right out the back door.

Hixon: Tyrone would lie through his teeth—and we'd believe him.

Sabatini: It was amazing how he tricked us. We were giving him money and buying him lunch. . . .

Hixon: And he'd sit there and say, "Oh, Mr. Officer, yes, I understand what you're saying. You're right. . . ."

Sabatini: Turn right around, and leave school.

Hixon: He was a good actor.

Sabatini: He slicked us.

Hixon: But you know what was amazing about Tyrone, after we really got to know him? Every time he'd try to do something bad, he'd bump right into us. . . .

Sabatini: Jumping from his mother's window . . .

Hixon: Right into our hands.

Sabatini: Poor guy.

Hixon: Remember when he cried at his house? He came across as so hard-core, so rough and tough out on the streets. But then one day we saw his mother spank him upstairs and he actually cried. And from that point on I took an interest in him.

Sabatini: He kept his front going all day long, but once his mom came home he was a horse of a different color.

Lloyd: Why do you think Tyrone did all those bad things?

Sabatini: To be honest with you, I just think he's a bad seed. I mean, he had a mother that cared, he had discipline, he had nice clothes, a decent place to live. . . .

Hixon: But he was from a broken home too. I mean, his father was incarcerated. . . .

Sabatini: Yeah, his father was abusive to his mother. . . . I don't know why Tyrone did what he did, really. But it was funny—the day after Eric got thrown out of the window, in roll call Hixon and I both said at the same time, "I bet Tyrone and Johnny did it." Didn't we?

Hixon: We sure did. It was amazing. And sure enough, it was.

Sabatini: And they had just been shooting off that gun the week before. We were in roll call and we heard these shots going off— and it was Johnny and Tyrone shooting at dogs on their way to school. How many times did we catch them with drugs and guns?

Hixon: Quite a bit.

Sabatini: Quite a few times with drugs and guns and stealing and lying and cutting school. Remember Tyrone's little brother, Roman? Right after the incident we had a candlelight vigil out in front of 3833 and hundreds of people marched all up and down The Wells with candles. Roman was there while we were lining up, and he kept telling everyone, "My name is Roman, and my brother is the one that threw the boy out the window." That's how he addressed himself to people. "What's your name?" "My name is Roman, and my brother's the one that threw the boy out the window." And finally I said, "You don't have to tell them all that. All you have to do is tell them your name. You are an individual and your brother is an individual, and what he did has no bearing on you." But that's how he introduced himself to people that night. I don't know why. . . . But Tyrone and Johnny—they were not your run-of-the-mill eleven-year-olds.

Hixon: I don't know if you ever met these guys, but Johnny was a little gangster. He was something. He would sit there and smirk in your face.

Sabatini: Both of them would.

Hixon: But Johnny had this look like he wanted to jump on you.

Sabatini: Yeah, he had that attitude. He was the leader, and Tyrone was the follower. Johnny was the instigator.

Hixon: He was just too far out there.

Sabatini: Way gone. Way gone.

Hixon: He was very hateful.

Sabatini: And Johnny's mother condoned his behavior. As long as that was the case, Johnny was going to keep on doing what he was doing.

Hixon: I did not like Johnny at all. But I liked Tyrone. Despite his problems. . . .

Sabatini: We liked him a whole lot. . . .

Hixon: I'll tell you what I liked about him. I saw he was a good kid that went bad. It became a challenge to me. I said, "I bet if this kid sticks by me I could get some sense in his head." And being a father, I could sense that he was just trying to reach out for help. . . .

Sabatini: Donnie has a son about Tyrone's age, so I think he saw something in Tyrone. . . .

Hixon: I knew that if he ever, ever, ever got out from under Johnny's spell, that he probably had a chance. But they'd been friends since kindergarten. That was the one thing that was strange to me—the relationship those two kids had. I mean, I had buddies when I was a kid, but those two—they were like Siamese twins. You did not see one without the other. It was unreal. They did everything together. Remember that girl they had over in the vacant apartment that gave them oral sex?

Lloyd: How old was she?

Hixon: She was their age, and there was a mattress in the apartment.

Sabatini: And there was that dog, General Grant. He was their companion. They'd all sleep together—that dog was bloody and flea-infested—and they would lay on that mattress with him in that vacant apartment and not come home all night.

Hixon: A lot of things we're discussing now were things that these guys did that were criminally wrong that never went on paper, because we were trying to give them the benefit of the doubt. And that's not unusual either. If a police officer catches a juvenile doing something, he's reluctant to arrest him.

Sabatini: Because nothing's going to be done.

Hixon: Boom—he's released.

Sabatini: No court date.

LeAlan: What do you think needs to be done to communities like The Wells to keep youth crimes from escalating?

Sabatini: I don't know what it's going to take. I think stricter penalties for juveniles would be nice. We need to lock them up. There's no punishment for juveniles unless they do something like Tyrone did. I think that if Tyrone and Johnny had been incarcerated after the first heroin incident, or the gun incident, or the other heroin incident, or the crack incident—this child probably would not have been killed.

Lloyd: If Tyrone would come back and beg for your help, would you help him?

Sabatini: No.

Hixon: Yeah.

Lloyd: If Tyrone got himself together and tried to apologize, and got a job and everything—what about then?

Sabatini: No. There's not enough apologizing in the world. What they did to that baby I wouldn't do to a roach. I hope that they both rot in hell.

133

Looking Out from 3833

CHAPTER 16

SHORTIES
IN THE 'HOOD

We did a lot of investigating around the 'hood, trying to find out about Eric, Derrick, Johnny, and Tyrone. We figured we'd probably recognize their faces from the projects—even though there's a lot of violence and fear here, most everyone is familiar with everyone else since people usually don't go too far from home.

Almost all of the shorties we talked to were touched in some way by the case. Like one afternoon we were playing Nintendo at Lloyd's house with some of his little buddies from The Wells. One of them, a nine-year-old named Antonio, told us he was with Eric right before he died.

Antonio: We was hanging out together—but I didn't go upstairs with him. I stayed downstairs.

LeAlan: So you were with him right before it happened?

Antonio: Yup. Then we saw the boys—Tyrone and his friends.

Lloyd: When they asked him to go up to the fourteenth floor, Eric didn't know what was fixing to happen, did he?

Antonio: Nope.

Lloyd: Did you see the body when it was on the ground?

Antonio: Yeah. He had blood on him. It looked ugly—for real.

LeAlan: Was he alive?

Hanging Out in Front of Lloyd's House

Antonio: Nope. He was dead.

Lloyd: Thank you very much. Signing off.

•　　　•　　　•

One day we were standing with our tape recorders outside 3833, and a little boy walked up to us. He told us he was ten years old, his name was Donell, and he knew Eric.

LeAlan: What is your relationship to Eric Morse?

Donell: He's my cousin.

LeAlan: How does it make you feel that your cousin is gone?

Donell: It makes me feel bad. I cry every night when I go to sleep. I just want him to be here now.

LeAlan: What are some of the things that you miss about your cousin?

Donell: I miss how he used to play with me. He used to always come over and play when I was alone or when my brother didn't want to play with me.

LeAlan: How much do you miss Eric?

Donell: More than I miss my own self.

LeAlan: What did you do when you first heard that your cousin was dead?

Donell: I started crying.

LeAlan: How long did you cry after Eric died?

Donell: About nine days.

LeAlan: What made you stop crying about him?

Donell: I stopped watching the news and I stopped crying. Every time he'd be on there I started crying.

LeAlan: Where were you at when you heard?

Donell: I seen it on the news. Every day I watch the news, so I found out.

LeAlan: Right now we're standing where Eric fell. See dirty baby Pampers, a foggy mist. You know this is where your cousin fell?

Donell: Yeah.

LeAlan: Do you know what happened?

Donell: The boy told Eric to go and steal some candy from the store. Eric said, "No." So he said, "Come on the fourteenth floor with me." And him and Derrick went up. And the first time Eric fell he didn't hurt himself, and then they took him back up there. . . .

137

Lloyd: Eric fell from the fourteenth floor and he didn't hurt himself?

Donell: Yeah. Then he went up there again and the boy bit Derrick's finger and Eric fell right there.

Lloyd: He died that time?

Donell: Yup. There goes his blood right there on the wall, under that window. Right there.

LeAlan: How does that make you feel?

Donell: Sad, man. I don't want to come over here no more. No more.

LeAlan: You think you could stay right here for about fifteen minutes and just think of Eric?

Donell: No!

Lloyd: You be ready to leave?

Donell: I be ready to cry. I'll start crying and then I'll start swinging.

LeAlan: Do you know the guys that did it?

Donell: Yeah, he goes to our school and I beat him up about five times for killing my cousin. His brother Roman goes to my school too. He lives right there.

LeAlan: What school do you go to?

Donell: Doolittle.

LeAlan: How do they look at you when they find out you're Eric Morse's cousin?

Donell: They start picking on me, so I beat 'em up.

LeAlan: Do you see Roman in school?

Donell: Yeah, I beat him up today.

LeAlan: You just violent, ain't you? You just beat up everybody.

Donell: Yup.

LeAlan: You think violence going to bring Eric back?

Donell: Nope. He ain't coming back.

LeAlan: Do you ever wish he'd come back?

Donell: Yeah.

LeAlan: Why?

Donell: So I can play with him again. He was fun. He wasn't nothing but five.

We asked Donell to come with us to find Tyrone's brother Roman. We found him playing in the parking lot behind one of the Darrow Homes.

·   ·   ·

Donell: Roman, come here. Run, Joe! Come on, I ain't going to touch you!

LeAlan: Hey, come here. No one's gonna hurt you. Let me talk to you. How old are you?

Roman: Nine.

LeAlan: You know what your brother did?

Roman: Nope.

Donell: Yes, you do!

Roman: I wasn't there.

LeAlan: You don't know he threw a little boy out the window?

Roman: That was Johnny.

Lloyd: Ain't your brother in jail for it?

Roman: My brother didn't do it. He's in jail 'cause he was with Johnny. He didn't throw him out the window—Johnny flipped him out the window! This is how it happened: I saw them coming over here and I heard Johnny say, "Let's go to this vacant apartment on the fourteenth floor." And they went upstairs. So at first they was planning on wrestling Eric. Then Johnny said, "Hey, Tyrone, we're going to flip Eric Morse out the window!" At first my brother was fixing to throw him out the window, then my brother helped him back up. Then Johnny said, "Look at them cats fighting." So Eric had to stand up on the banister to see, and Johnny just pushed him out the window. His shirt was up over his head. That's how it went.

Lloyd: Tyrone told you what had happened?

Roman: Yeah.

LeAlan: What did your brother used to do that made him bad?

Roman: He used to run away.

LeAlan: You ever steal with your big brother?

Roman: Nope.

LeAlan: Why?

Roman: 'Cause my brother didn't like me hanging with him.

LeAlan: Did you know Eric?

Roman: Yup. Him *and* Derrick. I used to been in their house every day. They was my best friends.

LeAlan: But yet you let your brother throw your friend out the window?

Roman: I didn't know they was going to do it. I found out after. Derrick came over there and said, "They threw my brother out the window."

Lloyd: You still love your brother?

Shorties in the 'Hood

Roman: Yeah, I love him.
LeAlan: All right, Shorty. . . .
Lloyd: Thanks.

•   •   •

Beautiful day outside. Walking around, keeping my eyes on every-thing. Little kids out here playing, flying kites, having life. I'm looking at the sky, thinking about Eric. Probably in heaven chilling with a lit-tle Tonka truck or something of that nature. Never know. There's a lot of nevers about Eric. Eric didn't even tip the coffee cup of life. What can you accomplish in five years? It takes more than five years to pay for a house. It takes more than five years to pay for a luxury car. More than five years to plan your twenty-fifth wedding anniversary. All Eric probably knew was the Ida B. Wells and the Darrow Homes. My bet is if you asked him to draw a picture of his life all you would see is dark-ness. What could he have painted a picture about?

Thinking about Tyrone and Johnny. They're victims too, if you think about it. They're going to have to keep hearing "Baby killers!" for the rest of their life. And when they get out they'll just be thugging again. All-American thugs is all they're ever gonna be if they don't ever see nothing but this.

Thinking about the Darrow Homes. The high-rises were built by Richard Daley's father so that the migrants from down South would be vertical instead of being spread out all over the city. Daley thought he was doing something great, but he's turning over in his grave now.

Now they're talking about tearing down all the high-rises and putting everyone in low-rise buildings as the solution. True, it's a start. But Tyrone and Johnny could have thrown Eric out of a vacant apartment in the low-rises and he could have fallen and broken his neck. So what are you going to do—make the low-rise homes lower? It's more than just the buildings. You don't know how it is to take a life until you value life itself. Those boys didn't value life. Those boys didn't have too much rea-son *to* value life. Now they killed someone and a part of them is dead too.

3833 at Night

CHAPTER 17

CLOSER THAN WE IMAGINED

We spent a lot of time trying to find ten-year-old Johnny's family. We heard they moved out of The Wells after the incident, but nobody in the neighborhood knew where they went. Then we got a tip that they moved in with Johnny's sister, Yvonne, in a project on the West Side of Chicago. Pretty soon we found the building and went over to find out what we could.

When we asked about the family at the security desk, we spotted our old friend from the Ida Bees, Little Wayne. We asked if he knew Johnny's sister, Yvonne. Little Wayne said that Yvonne was *his* sister also. Our homie Little Wayne was Johnny's older brother. Suddenly, we knew who Johnny was—the little light-skinned boy that used to follow Little Wayne around. I was shocked—I couldn't believe it!

We went upstairs with Little Wayne to try to interview his family, but they slammed the door in our face. So we talked to Little Wayne in a staircase outside his sister's apartment.

LeAlan: Why am I talking to you?
Little Wayne: About my little brother throwing the little boy out the window.
LeAlan: Do you know why he did it?
Little Wayne: No. I was over at my cousin's house when it happened.

When I was fixing to come home I saw the police. I ran upstairs and looked out the window. They had my brother, so I told my momma.

LeAlan: What happened, dog?

Little Wayne: I don't know. I can't go see him because I ain't old enough—I got to be twenty-one. I can't speak to him either.

LeAlan: You can't speak to your brother? How does that make you feel?

Little Wayne: Can't say. Can't say nothing.

LeAlan: How old are you?

Little Wayne: Fourteen.

LeAlan: Describe your little brother.

Little Wayne: He bad. He crazy.

Lloyd: Then you think your little brother did it?

Little Wayne: No, he ain't that crazy.

LeAlan: You say he crazy, but what were some fun things that you remember about your little brother?

Little Wayne: He used to help me fight, I used to help him fight. We did everything with each other.

LeAlan: Like a regular little brother?

Little Wayne: Yup.

LeAlan: When did Johnny start slipping?

Little Wayne: When he started hanging with Tyrone.

LeAlan: Why didn't you try to tell him not to hang with Tyrone?

Little Wayne: He didn't listen to me. He'll run out of the house, then we'll call the police and he'll come back and then run away again.

Lloyd: Did he sleep in the house?

Little Wayne: No.

LeAlan: So he was ten years old, outside kicking it by himself.

Little Wayne: With Ty.

LeAlan: How does it make your whole household feel when you bring up his name?

Little Wayne: I don't bring up his name when I'm in the house.

LeAlan: What's the mood in the house?

Little Wayne: Nothing. They just don't say nothing.

LeAlan: At night, when you sit down and think about it, do you ever shed tears about your little brother?

Little Wayne: Nah.

LeAlan: Why not?

Little Wayne: 'Cause I just be getting that off my mind.
Lloyd: You think you'll ever see him free?
Little Wayne: Probably will. I don't know.
LeAlan: So what have you learned from this?
Little Wayne: Nothing.
LeAlan: You just going to keep living your life.
Little Wayne: Yup.

•   •   •

What's up? This is LeAlan. It's ten o'clock and I'm in my bedroom, just thinking about the story. I guess I should have expected the unexpected with this one, but it's closer than I imagined. It's closer than I goddamned imagined! I knew Johnny. When people talk about him, really they're talking about one of my friends. No kid comes out like that—throwing a little baby out a fourteenth-story window! No way you can lay all the blame on Johnny and Tyrone. I'd say it's twenty-five percent blame for the kids, twenty-five percent blame for the parents, twenty-five percent blame for the building, and twenty-five percent blame for the environment—that equals a hundred percent failure!

Look at it. It's like cooking: If you put in sugar and apples and oranges and lemons, when you eat it it's going to be sweet. But if you put vinegar and sour stuff, it's going to be sour. You put in what you get out. And that's the case. These kids didn't have the right ingredients to be good kids, so you just can't expect any more than what's happened. And there's a lot of more kids out here like that. What else do you think would happen when they grow up in a concrete world? Think about it. The whole Ida B. Wells looks like a 1995 concentration camp. All you have is steel. Dirt and iron. Metal. That's all. Concrete and mortar. That's all. Nothing else. A kid deserves something better than that. *I* deserve better than that. I'm out of here. Peace.

Arlethea Morse

CHAPTER 18

REMORSE

An interview with Arlethea Morse:

LeAlan: *What was your relationship to Eric Morse?*
Arlethea Morse: Eric Morse was my nephew. His mother, Toni, is my sister. At the time of the incident Eric was five years old. He was a good little boy.

LeAlan: *What do you remember about Eric that sticks in your mind every time that you think of him?*
He was very intelligent, he was very playful. He could give you the details of everything from top to bottom. I remember when he used to tell me about movies—his brother Derrick would try to explain the movie, and Eric would say, "No, the movie didn't go like that, Auntie Letha, the movie went like this. . . ." And he would tell me every little detail from top to bottom. Then I'd watch the movie, and he was always correct. And Eric *did not lie.* If you wanted to know the exact truth about exactly how something went, ask Eric and he would tell you. If anybody did anything wrong, he'd say, "I'm going to tell!" And he would tell. And this is the reason I think those boys killed him. After we went and told Tyrone's momma what was going on with stealing the candy, those boys got angry. They took Eric and Derrick up to the fourteenth floor and started hitting Derrick in his chest to

terrorize him. But they couldn't terrorize Eric—because *Eric was going to tell.* They had scared Derrick, but they *could not* scare Eric. No one could scare Eric. So they held him out the window that first time to scare him, and he was *still* going to tell. And I guess they really didn't want him to tell.

Lloyd: *What are some of your worries about Derrick?*
That's kind of hard to say, because Derrick was Eric's brother and Derrick and Eric were very close. For a while he was always saying, "Baby going bye-bye." And that used to worry me a whole lot. Like if you'd say the name Eric when you meant to say Derrick, he would say, "Baby going bye-bye." Or he'd be sitting on the couch and he'd just say, "Baby going bye-bye." The first time we actually heard that he was in the tub taking a bath, and I asked him did he need a towel and he told me, "Yes," and I gave him a towel. He said, "Auntie Letha?" and I said, "What, baby?" And he said, "Baby going bye-bye." And I said, "O.K." and I walked away and I thought, "I wonder what he meant by that?" And I asked him and he said he meant that the baby's gone and he's never going to come back. And then what really hurt my heart was when we had the funeral and Derrick went up and saw Eric's body. When we went outside and got in the car he said, "Auntie Letha, who was that?" I said, "That was your brother." He said, "He didn't look like that." And I said, "Well, baby." I just rocked him. I said, "After that hard fall it kind of damaged him a little bit, but that was your brother." That's one moment that really hurt my heart. That was his brother. I don't know what to say about it. . . . You know it's still . . . I can't . . . I can't say how he's going to be. I don't think any of us will ever get over it. We'll always remember him. He was a good little boy. He was. It's been very bad for the whole family, especially Eric's little cousins and nieces and nephews. They're just not right. They're all rebellious now, they always have something bad to say to other kids, they all want to fight. But we try to keep them in check. The anniversary of Eric's death is coming up, so we'll have a little cake and ice cream and take out the pictures and sit back and talk about Eric. He is not forgotten.

Lloyd: *What do you think of the little kids that committed the crime?*
What do I think of them? Well, I knew little Tyrone and I knew

Johnny. I used to take Johnny to the lake. I used to give him candy. He used to have dogs and I used to feed his dogs. So it hurt my heart when I found out what they had done. But they were just being kids with no discipline, so I don't have anything bad to say about them. And really I don't have hatred in my heart for the parents either. I think the kids need help and I think the families need help also. That's the way I see it.

Lloyd: *Thank you very much, Arlethea Morse.*

•　　　•　　　•

We waited almost a year for an interview with Eric's mother, Toni, and his nine-year old brother, Derrick. Their attorney told us that out of all the requests from across the country, this was the only interview they were granting to anyone in the media. We got to talk to Toni and Derrick for about twenty minutes.

Lloyd: What do you best remember about Eric?

Toni: He liked to play. He liked to flip a lot. . . .

LeAlan: Like on those old beds, those box springs? That's how we used to do it.

Toni: No, not on a box spring. He just flipped. Him and his brother used to do that a lot.

LeAlan: What is one of your fondest memories of Eric that doesn't leave your mind?

Toni: He just kept me laughing, always saying little humorous things. I always think about him. There's not a day that goes past that I don't think about my child. He kept me smiling and laughing, and that just kept me going on in life.

LeAlan: Before the days of October, was there any omens to indicate anything like this would happen?

Toni: No.

Lloyd: How did you first hear what happened?

Toni: Derrick came to me. He said, "Momma, Eric is hurt." I said, "How is he hurt?" He said, "The little boys threw him out the window." And I just started screaming. . . .

LeAlan: Do you know the young men that did it?

Toni: No. My sister knew them, and that's how I went over to their house. I never did know the little boys, period.

Toni Morse

Lloyd: What do you think of the kids?

Toni: I don't hate them. I just hate what they did to my child.

LeAlan: Do you feel any animosity toward the parents of the young men for allowing them to do such a thing?

Toni: I just feel sorry for them for raising their kids like that. There has to be something wrong with them to throw a child out the window. Got to be something wrong with *anybody* to do something like that!

Lloyd: What kind of future do you think those little children will have?

Toni: Not very much of a future.

LeAlan: Ms. Morse, how do you think Derrick's changed since the incident?

Toni: His behavior has changed since the incident. He likes to fight now. [To Derrick] Tell them you rebellious. You like to fight people now.

Derrick: Fight. Throw crayons.

Toni: He likes to fight—something he never did. Because at one time he wouldn't fight—him or Eric—they would run from people. Maybe he's lashing out.

Lloyd: You get your anger out by fighting?

Derrick: Sometimes.

LeAlan: What grade are you in?

Derrick: Fourth.

LeAlan: How do you feel toward the young men that did this?

Derrick: Bad.

LeAlan: How has life been for you after this?

Derrick: Sad.

Lloyd: If you had one more day to spend with your brother, what would you do?

Derrick: Go swimming and play with him a lot.

LeAlan: Where do you feel your brother's at now?

Derrick: In heaven.

LeAlan: Is he still your little brother, or your big brother 'cause he high up?

Derrick: Little.

Lloyd [to Toni]: Does he ever talk about his brother?

Toni: Of course. We always talk about him. I want him to talk about him for the rest of his life.

LeAlan: If you had one more thing to say to Eric, what would it be?

Toni: That I love him and miss him. . . . I miss him being around, making me laugh. Miss putting his clothes on, miss hugging him—a lot of little things. But I'm strong—I have to be strong for Derrick. I just miss his little butt, that's all.

Lloyd: How long do you think it will take for the wounds to heal?

Toni: Probably never.

• • •

The trial of Johnny and Tyrone started on October 17, 1995. I was in court that day. Johnny walked in first—he was light-skinned and looked a lot like his brother Little Wayne. Then Tyrone came in—his hair was sticking up all wild. There was a guard with him, and when the door slammed behind them Tyrone jumped like he was real nervous or traumatized. Supposedly during the hearing Johnny was mouthing swear words at people in the courtroom. I didn't see that. All I know is that at one point Johnny turned around, looked directly at me, and gave a head nod—he recognized me from the 'hood. I gave him one right back, and he turned back around. That was it.

The next day, both of the boys were found delinquent (that's what they call "guilty" in Juvenile Court) of first-degree murder. The prosecution and defense argued for months about the punishment. Before this case, the maximum punishment in Illinois for children younger than thirteen was probation and counseling. After the murder of Eric Morse, the Illinois legislature made a new law saying that children as young as ten could be locked up in youth prison.

On January 29, 1996, Judge Carol Kelly handed down her decision. She sentenced Johnny and Tyrone to prison, making them the nation's youngest inmates. Tyrone and Johnny are now incarcerated in separate juvenile prisons in Illinois, where they could remain until they are twenty-one.

The same week that Johnny and Tyrone were sentenced, our friend Little Wayne, Johnny's brother, was arrested for the criminal sexual assault of a four-year-old girl. We'll probably never see him again. And we'll probably never get to meet Johnny and Tyrone face-to-face. Their lawyers didn't let us interview them because they're minors. But Johnny's lawyer did say that Johnny knows just what we've done. He told us Johnny cut our picture out of the newspaper and has it hanging over his bed in the prison. I guess we must symbolize something to him—what he could have been or what he should have been. I wish him all the hope in the world.

•   •   •

Hello, diary. It's me, LeAlan, sitting here reflecting on a tragedy. A year has passed since we started the story, and nothing has changed in the Ida B. Wells. Most people don't even remember Eric anymore. If we lived in China there would probably be a vigil or a ceremony, but here it ain't nothing. I just hope people can learn something from what we've done. People shouldn't take this case at face value. At first they might have said, "These little kids are killers—look at them!" But you got to think: They were young and they lived in a savage environment. Look what happened.

I have a nephew that's five and another nephew that's three, and I'd hate to see something happen to them, but I couldn't get mad at the perpetrators if they were brought up in this environment. It's like a lion. A lion is raised up to kill 'cause if he don't kill, he don't eat. These kids are brought up with that same mentality.

The whole thing is totally wrong. The University of Chicago is walking distance from the Ida B. Wells. It has some of the greatest Nobel Prize winners of this last century, nuclear physicists that almost cracked the atom—but kids around here don't even know it's there. Some kids have never even been downtown. They only know what they've seen in the Ida B. Wells. So I just can't blame them entirely for doing what they did. I can't hold them accountable for that.

Violence breeds violence in The Wells. It's like a chameleon that changes colors to adapt to its environment—when these kids are surrounded by violence they become violent also. Or like the Blob—when it touches you it sucks you in and it just keeps getting bigger and bigger. When it started, the Blob was little. It ate the first guy, it got a little bit bigger. It ate the second guy, it got a little bit bigger. Ate the third guy and got bigger. And by the end of the movie the Blob was huge. When young people around here are touched by violence, it changes their whole persona. And if there's no reform, there's going to be more and more violence.

Kids around here have got to have more things to do. They need counseling. Get the teachers to put more emphasis on teaching them how to love and respect one another before they start teaching them

153

Eric Morse (far left), February 17, 1989–October 13, 1994

how to add and subtract—because if the kids are violent and show no respect, how can they learn anything?

Some way, somehow, we've got to turn this whole thing around into a positive. I got hope though, 'cause two negatives make a positive. That's what I learned in math the other day. I'll leave you on that note. Peace.

PART III

LIFE—1996

Lloyd's Niece Rere

CHAPTER 19

THE MAZE

LeAlan: It's Thursday, the twelfth of September 1996. It's me and my partner in crime, Lloyd Newman, catching you up on some things that have happened since we told you about our lives in 1993. Talk about yourself, Lloyd.

Lloyd: I'm seventeen, a junior at Future Commons High School. Could be doing better, but I'm gonna get it together.

LeAlan: And I'm seventeen years old and a senior at Martin Luther King High School. Varsity football and baseball captain, on my way to college just a few months from now. So one thing I want to talk about is the neighborhood and how it has changed. It *has* changed.

Lloyd: The fighting, the violence.

LeAlan: It was a lot cooler back in '93.

Lloyd: In school I wrote a story about how living in the projects is like being in a big maze that you almost can't get out of.

LeAlan: That's the truth. It's like you're in this maze, and you either die in it or you escape. Right now I'm probably close to getting out. But you never know—it could be a trap. I might take that wrong turn and be right back at the beginning again. I don't know. But I sit here, you know, and a lot of people might look at our situation as being terrible, but the terrible thing about it is I can't say it's all bad.

Lloyd: It ain't all bad. You have some people out here who are good. But I think that if people keep messing up, by the year 2000 everybody will be either dead or out on the corner.

LeAlan: True. I mean with them cutting off welfare, a lot of these shorties are going to be even more messed up.

Lloyd: That's the worst thing you could do—cut off aid around the projects!

LeAlan: Shorties are going to be out here starving, and they're going to want to eat. It's going to be hell out here!

Lloyd: It's going to be war.

LeAlan: An apocalypse!

Lloyd: Shorties are going to be sticking up.

LeAlan: It's going to be unreal! But I've been thinking about this: Why are we dependent on other folks to take care of us? Why can't we be independent instead of dependent? I know I just couldn't sit around all month waiting for a check. I mean, if you're a grown, able-bodied adult you should be working. So I think of that—but then I think of these little shorties when welfare gets cut off. . . .

Lloyd: And all the mothers who have little children. It ain't right.

LeAlan: But think of this: If I was hungry, would you feed me a fish?

Lloyd: Yeah. . . .

LeAlan: Or would you teach me how to fish so I wouldn't be hungry anymore?

Lloyd: I'd teach you how to fish.

LeAlan: Right. Because if I'm used to you giving me this fish, when you're gone I can't eat.

Lloyd: But you can't just let people starve. . . .

LeAlan: True. So I'd feed them that first day, but then teach them so they could do if for themselves.

Lloyd: Right. People out here want to learn, they're just getting taught the wrong things. Yesterday I caught this six-year-old boy smoking a cigarette—I wanted to smack him!

LeAlan: But the sad thing is that these shorties out here are *smart*. That's what kills me.

Lloyd: They're smart!

LeAlan: But it's like crabs in a crab barrel—you got one crab trying to get out, and the others pull him down. Around here, when someone tries to make it out, everyone tries to pull him back in, and he's not strong enough to fight them off. Just think of our eighth-grade class—all the people that were smart back then are out here dealing now.

Lloyd: Every last one of them.

LeAlan: Every last one of them. It's only about . . . let me see . . . fifteen percent of us who are doing something with our lives: me, you, your brother Mike—that's it. Everybody else is messing up. And I'm not saying this just to scare people—it's the truth.

Lloyd: Sure is.

LeAlan: But I *still* can't say living around here is all bad. If I say that the community I live in is sad, that means my life is sad—and that's not true. I have a prosperous life—have a car, play ball . . .

Lloyd: But no matter what you accomplish, you're going to die.

LeAlan: That's true—I can sit out here and be a thug and die or I could be a lawyer and die. Either way I'm going to die. But the point is how fast and how quick.

Lloyd: The point is how you live your life.

LeAlan: Just think how many people have died out here since '93. There is nothing here that's permanent. We're all temporary. It's like we're working a part-time job—because life isn't full-time.

Lloyd: I wish it was, though. Would you want to live forever?

LeAlan: No, I wouldn't. And I know I'm not coming back either.

Lloyd: You're not coming back, so you better have fun while you're here. Hey, LeAlan, how would this world be with nothing?

LeAlan: Be like it was before.

Lloyd: I'm talking about nothing. No buildings, nobody—nothing!

LeAlan: It would be a peaceful place—that's all I can say.

Lloyd: That's the most peaceful place you can get.

LeAlan: True. . . . Hey, kid, I'm sleepy now, so we'll leave on that note. I'm out.

Mrs. Helen Finner

CHAPTER 20

THE 'HOOD

Our neighborhood has changed for the worse since we did *Ghetto Life 101* in '93—for the *ultimate* worse. The violence and killing are out of control. In the summer of '96, we had our first major gang war in The Wells in years. Everyone around here was scared.

To find out more about the situation, we talked to Helen Finner, who's been president of the Ida B. Wells tenant organization for twenty-three years and has lived in The Wells since 1968.

LeAlan: *Mrs. Finner, how has The Wells changed since you moved here?*
From good to bad. When I came here, The Wells was the prettiest place I ever moved to in my life—I thought I had moved into heaven. All the kids played, you could sit out on your porch all night long. Now it's almost like living in hell. Especially with the gang war that's going on now. Last week I was standing on my front porch and got shot. I could have been killed but I was lucky—the bullet just skinned my ankle. So the community is running scared, but now it's too late. We've let this war get a grip on us.

Lloyd: *What problems have made Wells what it is now?*
Gangs. Drugs. And the main thing is no jobs. All the young men standing around that are involved in gangs wouldn't be a problem if they had jobs. Once a young man gets involved in gangs there is no returning—there's no way out but death. And I've seen it happen. I

The Eric Morse Basketball Hoop

went to two funerals yesterday. Just *yesterday*. And these were good kids. You know, sometimes I get so angry when I'm talking, because I look at all these kids and I wonder, "How many are going to grow up into men and women?" Lives are snatched just like that around here. I fear for these children every day. Every day.

And the parents are afraid of their children. If you would just come to my office and sit with me for one day, you'd see how many mothers bring their kids over. "Can you talk to my child?" Because they are afraid of them. They are afraid of their *own children*. I'm not afraid of any kids. I don't have sense enough to be afraid.

LeAlan: *How did you feel about the incident in 3833?*
It was the most horrible thing I ever witnessed in my life. I could not believe it when I saw that baby laying on the ground dead. And everybody made such a big commotion—you saw so many TV cameras here that week, running all around the Darrow Homes taking pictures, interviewing everybody. But who's in here interviewing the ones that have been killed lately? Nobody. Nobody comes here now. The people that got shot on Saturday weren't even in the newspapers. It's ridiculous! See, Eric became a martyr. He became a symbol. But even then, nothing's been done for him. Some kind of memorial should have been set up to remember that this little boy's life was taken from him before his time. They should rename the Darrow Homes for him.

Lloyd: *They named a basketball hoop in the Darrow Homes for him.*
What good is it? Who's playing on it? Is anybody playing basketball over there? No. Why? 'Cause they can't. It's too dangerous. It's ridiculous.

LeAlan: *How does it make you feel when you know that the building where he was thrown from . . .*
Is gonna get torn down at long last? You know what? If I had my way, I would empty the buildings out right now and hurry up and knock all four of 'em down and start a new beginning. That's what it's gonna take—a new beginning.

To tell you the truth, I'm sick of it. I'm on the verge of giving up and moving out—it's gotten *that bad* with me. It's like I'm fighting a losing battle every day. We need help. Someone needs to hear our cry.

Tearing Down the Darrow Homes

CHAPTER 21

SCHOOL

In the summer of '96 we also went back to Donoghue Elementary School to see how things were going. We found our principal, Ms. Margaret A. Tolson, still in charge at the school.

LeAlan: *How have the last three years been since the class of '93 left Donoghue?*
Ms. Tolson: The last three years have been exciting but difficult. There have been a lot of changes in the community and a lot of changes with the students. Not all for the best. There's a lot more violence now than there was in '93. In '93 it was not the case of police coming to school to take you out. This school year we have had the police coming into the building on several occasions to take children out, and it's been a matter of talking to them and saying, "This is how you act when the police pick you up. No, you will not give them lip and you will not give them resistance." And parents have begun to understand the need to keep our records current so that when those children are taken we can contact someone. We've also had a couple of stabbings. And the difficult thing about it has been when you return the child who was stabbed to the same classroom with the child who did the stabbing, it's difficult to ask them to concentrate on what they need to concentrate on.

Lloyd: *What do you remember about our class?*
What do I remember about your class? I remember that you were a

Ms. Tolson and Student

group of very creative individuals. And I do mean *individuals*. Each one of you was distinctly different. You didn't believe that you really needed all of the education that we were trying to give. You were convinced that you knew it all, and that you could have taught the class, run the building, and gotten it all done better than we could.

Your class had a lot of private and personal battles. I remember a lot of students who worked hard at Donoghue, but for whom their freshman year of high school was a very bad year. I recall seeing some late at night on the street with police officers and stopping to say, "Are you all right?" And them saying, "I can handle it." So I think your class had to grow up fast.

LeAlan: *It's now 1996. You said in '93 that only about five or six percent of our class would not make it. Right now where do you think that percentage is?*
That's difficult, and it's difficult because it takes time with some of you. What I like to emphasize is that learning is a lifelong process. And I would say the percentage of students who will end up making it from your class is probably fifty percent. A good half of them are going to make it and do well. They won't all make it at the same time—some of those who are now dealing drugs and fighting with the law need to learn their lessons, and as they learn those life lessons, they'll make changes and turn themselves around. It may take them until they're twenty-five or thirty before they make that decision, but they will make it.

LeAlan: *Is there anyone who you can look at now who you felt was very bleak back then but has changed around?*
I can look at Lloyd, because he was very quiet until you two started doing the interviews. He didn't have a lot to say in classes. He was the little person people would push in corners and say, "As long as he doesn't cause a problem we can pass him along." Lloyd is one of the children I would have had a question mark about. But at this point I think he's going to make it. I have no problem saying he's going to make it. He's definitely going to make it.

LeAlan: *How does it make you feel when you see that the violence is increasing? How does it make you feel as a principal and a person that's* *trying to help kids in life but you can't be around them twenty-four hours a day to shelter them from what they see?*

It makes me feel as if I need to convince parents that they've got to take some time with their children. The majority of my children are more satisfied with a hug than they are with a buck. They want the closeness. They want somebody who cares about them.

Donoghue is in a war zone. Our children here have some of the same symptoms that you see if you look at children who live in war zones in Africa. When my children have heard shooting all night and they come here in the morning and they're tired and sleepy—that's living in a war zone. When they're dodging bullets—that's living in a war zone. When they know they'll be beaten going from one gang area to the next when they walk to school—that's living in a war zone. It's that kind of thing that should not be. It simply shouldn't be. But it's there. And somehow we have to get the children who live in this war zone to feel that life is worthwhile. But I'm here to fight the battle. I'm here with teachers who are willing to fight the battle. We won't give up on you. We can't give up.

You see, if nothing else, the children of Donoghue are survivors. They may go through trials and they may go through tribulations, but they survive. And once they have survived, watch out—there's no telling where they can go! They will be strong and they will be able to meet the future—whatever it brings. I'm very proud of you two. Tell the world to watch out, because I may be talking to the next President of the United States and his Secretary of State.

Lloyd: *Thank you very much, Ms. Tolson.*

•   •   •

In 1996, the Chicago Board of Education enforced new rules saying that students had to make at least a 6.8 grade level in reading and math to move on to high school. This past year, only eleven out of the forty kids in the eighth-grade class at Donoghue had high enough scores to graduate. Now the school has been put on probation. If the test scores don't come up, the Board might remove Ms. Tolson and all of the teachers, or even close Donoghue down completely.

But whatever happens, I will never forget Donoghue or our eighth-grade class. We did a lot of stuff together—we climbed through ceilings, we trashed classrooms—we were wild! We were wild, and we

170

were smart. And now most of us are just doing what society wants us to do—contributing to the jail population, selling drugs, having babies, living on welfare. But I know I'll never turn my back on the kids I grew up with. We went through a lot together!

June Jones

CHAPTER 22

LeALAN

What's up? LeAlan Jones here. Almost four years have passed since you first heard my voice. When we made *Ghetto Life 101* I was thirteen years old, about four foot two and 115 pounds. I was in eighth grade then—a little man. I don't consider myself a little guy anymore. One thing that makes me older is my mental state— I listen to jazz, read, try to educate my mind. I'm seventeen now, doing well, and everybody tells me, "You're gonna be this!" and "You're gonna be that!" But that's scary in a way. It's a lot of stress thinking about the possibility of not making it. So I still work constantly. It's like swimming. While you're working you're going to stay afloat, but the minute you stop moving is the minute you start sinking. When you think you're comfortable is when you drown. I'm never going to drown!

My family is doing well too. Since '93 my mom hasn't had a mental relapse and my sister, Janell, has calmed down. In September 1996, my grandmother and my grandfather celebrated their fiftieth wedding anniversary. They had a big party and renewed their vows to each other at church. My grandfather is now almost completely recovered from the strokes he had back in '89, and has a much easier time talking. I interviewed both of my grandparents one Saturday night in their bedroom.

Hello. Today I'm here with . . .
June: June Marie Jones, your grandmother, and your grandfather Gussie Lee Jones.

Gus Jones

What are we going to talk about?
June: About the neighborhood and how it's changed since 1993.

How has it changed?
June: The most significant change that I have seen is the gang-wars. There's more drug activity, more drive-by shootings, and more innocent people being killed. I see no improvement. I only see negative things happening now. And with the cutting off of people's public aid and SSI, basically I don't see any hope for the people around here.

What are some of the improvements that you have seen in the last three years?
June: Well. . . . They're tearing down some of the developments that need to be torn down. . . . And with the Democratic Convention this summer they redid King Drive and put little golden plaques with different black people's names on them, and they have new shrubbery and cute little benches for people to sit on while they are waiting for the bus. So that's an improvement.

What good experiences have you had in the last few years?
June: Oh, that's a tough question. Just being alive is good. Our family having good health and no major sicknesses. And my fiftieth wedding anniversary—that was a beautiful occasion.

How did you and Granddaddy stay together for fifty years?
June: Hell if I know. [She laughs]
Gus: I always let her have her way. I never interfered in her having her way. I never judged her in no form or fashion.
June: He knew it wasn't going to do no good to tell me what to do anyway, because I have a mind of my own.

Grandaddy, what changes have you seen in me since I was young?
Gus: Well, LeAlan, you never did appear like no other boys to me. When you were about eleven I would sit on the porch and listen to you talk, and you would say things that were just amazing to me. I couldn't do nothing but sit there and look at you. You are a smart boy. You are smart!

How does it make you feel that I'll be going away to college?
Gus: It makes me feel ten feet tall, LeAlan. And I'm still growing! Everything you do, every attempt you make to climb higher, I feel taller. Every time I see you going higher, I go higher. It makes me grow a little bit every day.

How did it make you feel bringing me on the airplane to go down to Orlando to give that speech a while back?
Gus: That made me feel good. Made me feel good! How many miles to get to Orlando?

Five or six hundred miles.
Gus: Five or six hundred miles? That whole trip was a joy. In the airport you walked so fast I couldn't keep up with you. I knew where you were going but I couldn't keep up with you, you were walking so fast. You were going out of sight. Out of sight. But then I knew you had been taught right when you slowed down to wait for me. You didn't walk off from me. I knew then that you were going the right way.

What advice would you give me for next year when I'm at college and I don't have you around?
June: I feel that wherever you are, I'll be there. Not in body, but I'll be there. And the things that I have tried to teach you have caught hold of you. I know looking at how you are now that my efforts were not in vain. Like Martin Luther King said, "I've been to the top of the mountain with you." So you have to carry on from here by yourself. And I know that you can make it.

What advice can you give me, Granddaddy?
Gus: The same advice I've always given you, LeAlan, is the advice I would give you now. Do not stop learning. Learning is the greatest form of happiness known to man. If you learn one thing, let that be a stepping-stone to learn some more. Every book you can find—read it. Keep on studying and keep on learning.

What do you see in my future?
June: I see very good things for you. I don't know if you will continue with this kind of work or not, but as I've said before: No matter what

you do you will be running your mouth. You've come far, and I believe that you will continue to do good work—whatever you choose to do with your life.

Are there any concluding thoughts that you would like to talk about here?
June: Not really—just to take life one day at a time. Because tomorrow is not promised to you. Tomorrow may never come, so just ask for the strength to do what you can on *this* day. One day at a time.

Thank you.

•　　　•　　　•

What's up, y'all? This is LeAlan Jones and I just feel like talking tonight. I got a lot of energy. Thinking about my life. I mean, it's ironic. Here I am, seventeen years old, and I take business trips for the weekend, speak on the same stage as Hillary Clinton, fly back home, and go to school the next day. I grew up in the ghetto, got an uncle and a cousin who are career criminals, no father, a mother who was pronounced mentally ill, a grandmother who raised damn near twenty children, a sister who had a baby at fifteen—but yet, I'm still making it. That's a testament to giving a person an opportunity and letting them make something of it. And the sad thing about it is that there's a lot more people out here just like me. But it's like they're in shallow quicksand and don't realize that it's not too deep to survive. All they've got to do is stand up. But people get scared and give up. The streets just suck them in like a Hoover vacuum cleaner and spit them back out.

I'm five foot seven and 147 pounds. I live in the ghetto. I'm supposed to be a loser. I'm supposed to be on the six o'clock news shooting people's heads off. I'm supposed to be the one that you grab for your purse when I walk by. I'm the person that doesn't vote. I'm the person that is supposed to drink. I'm the person that is supposed to smoke weed. I'm the motherfucker that is supposed to fill your jails. I'm the person that you make examples to your kid of what not to be like. I'm supposed to be a basketball player. I'm supposed to make it only because of affirmative action. I'm not supposed to be positive. I'm not supposed to be educated. I'm not supposed to know what I know. But I do.

I just sit back and contemplate: Why did things turn out this way? Why have I been given these opportunities? Why will I probably

Tootchie Jones

make it out of here while others won't? Why? I don't know. This world is a funny, perplexing place. I'm going to leave on that thought. Peace.

•   •   •

A few words with my mother, Tootchie:

So what have you been doing in the last three years? Any relapses?
No, because I'm on my medication. I take my medication and I feel better and I think better.

What are some of your greatest experiences in the last three years?
Two years ago I flew to New York to get an award with you. Flying is something I said I'd never do, but we flew to New York and I wasn't afraid—I just wanted to try it. They had salmon at the awards ceremony, but I didn't eat it.

How did being a reporter change me?
I think we were closer before. We used to talk about your homework, and we don't do that anymore. I'm not as close to you as I'd like to be. But I think you are growing. You are seventeen now, a young man, and I think you are doing great academically and spiritually.

What type of person do you think I am overall?
I think you should have your blood pressure checked because you got a lot of stress and your nose bleeds. You need to stop getting so hyper and take things more calmly. You are not calm.

If I don't make it, will you be disappointed?
No, I wouldn't be disappointed. I know that you did all you can do. If you don't make it, I'm going to still love you and keep encouraging you to go farther.

How do you feel about me going to college?
I hope you don't call home collect.

That's my mother. Peace.

•   •   •

My sister, Janell, is doing better too, even though it took her a little while. In '94 she moved out of our house and got her own place in a

Janell Jones Smoking

project near us called Stateway Gardens. It's not a great apartment—on the top floor with rats running through it—but she's done her best to make it a home. There's a lot of holes in the walls from a violent boyfriend she had staying with her—he used to beat her pretty bad. And a year ago Janell was seriously assaulted by another ex-boyfriend who had just gotten out of prison. So it hasn't been an easy time for her. But somehow Janell has begun to turn her life around. In the past year she got herself a job at McDonald's and started taking computer classes at a technical institute. Now she's getting ready to take the test for the GED. I'm very proud of her.

Since 1993 what are some of things that have changed in your life?
Janell: I think I'm doing a little bit better. I don't drink as much as I used to. I've been doing more thinking than I was a couple of years ago. I try to spend more time with my son and help him read. I try to help my grandmomma and do other little things to help keep me busy so I won't have to be out there in the street—because it ain't nice out there.

Who do you think helped change your life around?
I did it myself mostly. I mean, I had encouragement from a lot of people, but mostly I had to put my mind to it and do it myself—because can't nobody change me but me.

How do you think your son changed you?
He stopped me from lying. He asks me questions about everything—like my drinking—and if I lie he always figures it out. He's big enough now to know when stuff ain't right and how people should act. So I can't be acting like I used to act—because I don't want him to start acting like that.

What do you think the future holds for him?
My baby is going to be great. He's going to get a good education and my baby is *not* going to be sitting around here selling drugs or holding a gun on anybody. He is *not* going to be like that—if I have to move out of this whole country and go somewhere else to keep him away from it!

If you could tell the President of the United States about your community, what would you tell him?

Janell and the Jones Dog, Ferocious

Well, let me see. . . . I think If people didn't feel like they were behind bars when they were walking outside at night, a lot of things would be different. I think what we need is to get people together and clean up around here so they can feel that they're doing something good at least for once in their life. See, there are a lot of bad people around here but there are a lot of good people too. It's just that it's hard to find anybody doing good—I guess because they feel ashamed that they aren't doing what everybody else is doing.

What do you think has happened to most of the guys in this community since 1993?
Most of them are dead—killing each other for no reason. There's been a lot of people that got killed, girls and boys, and that's a shame.

What do you think the reason is behind that?
Jealousy. People sell drugs and make their fast money, and other people get jealous and just shoot them for the hell of it. They really don't have any reason to be doing what they are doing—it's all stupid.

What do you see yourself doing in the next three or four years?
I plan by January to have my GED, and then start working at the post office. Maybe within the next eight to ten months I should be moving out of Stateway and finding an apartment somewhere better.

From running in the streets like you used to do to what you are doing now, what advice could you give a young female teenager?
Don't do it. Believe me. It seems like it's fun at the time, but you have to think about what's going to happen after you get through. I just wish that I would have stayed in school. It ain't no fun waiting once a month for that little check that the government gives you, and then you try to get a job and you can't. Just do what your parents tell you. My mistake is that I started listening too late.

Take your time—you will get there. If people want to help you—as long as they aren't doing anything to hurt you or your baby—listen to them. Take everything slow. Don't rush anything, especially if you aren't sure about something. The more that you rush, the more you are going to have to end up going back and repeating what you've already done. Just take your time.

183

June Jones

LᴇALAN

*What is the one single thing that you would like to let everybody know
about people who live in the situation that we do?*
It's hard living around here. It is. Because if you're trying to make honest money and not just dealing drugs, people are always trying to take
what you've got. And you get judged differently by living around here.
Like me, if I try to apply for a job and I use my address, they will not
hire me. I can't really explain how it is, because you'd have to be here.
I can't say, "Come visit," because it wouldn't be no good to visit. You'd
have to live here to see how it really is, and you wouldn't want to do
that either. So I'll just say it ain't easy.

Thank you.

Lloyd

CHAPTER 23

LLOYD

Let me see. . . . Since 1993, we moved into a better apartment in The Wells. My sister Precious got a job working in the little corner store and had her second baby—Rockell. My sister Sophia is doing the same as she was. Right now both of them are pregnant. My father, Chill—he's the same. And me myself—I'm doing much better. I got dreams—go to college, move my family away from here, be rich and famous, maybe own a hardware store. I'll be anything that I can be to help me stay off the streets and take care of myself and my family.

But I got to go to school. I haven't been doing good in school—it just seems like I'm too tired to do anything. I have to get my mind focused and stop listening to myself— because I send myself the wrong way sometimes. But now I'm going to start doing my homework and pay more attention to what people are trying to tell me. It isn't hopeless. I'll go to summer school and regular school and night school—I'll never drop out. I don't care how long it takes, I'm going to make it!

I interviewed my sister Sophia about how her life has changed over the last four years.

Hello, this is Lloyd Newman interviewing Sophia Newman. What's happened since 1993?
Sophia: Things seem to be the same. I'm still not happy like I'm supposed to be. I just get through the days. Mostly I just wake up every

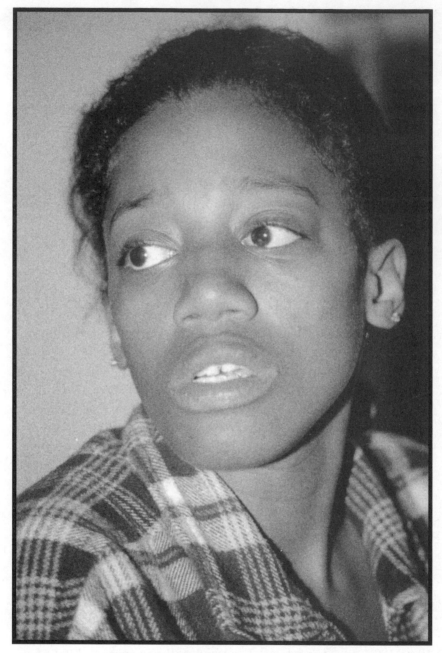

Sophia Newman

day and do the same thing: get out of bed, put on clean clothes, and stay in the house. I never go outside. There's nowhere to go. Sometimes people say, "You never leave the house!" And I'm like, "For what? There ain't nothing to do."

Let me see. . . . Precious had another baby—Rere. Now she's got another one on the way. And I just found out that I'm pregnant with my first child. It took me by shock at first, but now I'm O.K. with it. What else?. . . . A couple of years ago our best friends died. Mark and Marvin. They were gunned down in front of their house on Christmas Day. They were twins, and their birthday is February 19—the same day as Rere was born.

What's happened with Chill?
He's the same. I can't say he's doing better, because he's still drinking. . . .

Been in and out of rehab . . .
Chill's always going to be the same. I don't think he's ever going to change. Seems like he wants to drink himself to death. He says he wants to be with Momma, so I guess that's what he's doing.

What about me?
I don't know. You're doing bad in school, but I ain't worried. One day you're going to realize that acting up in school isn't worth it and get yourself together. You've always been hardheaded, even when Momma was living. You always say to us, "You're not my mother!" We know we're not your mother. We're not trying to take the place of Momma. We're just trying to help lead you in the right way. You don't realize that, but you're going to wake up. And I don't care if it takes an extra year, you're going to pull through school. So I ain't too much worried about you. I don't got time to be worried about you—I have enough headache as it is.

Do you think you've been a good mother to us?
Yes. I was only seventeen when Momma died. Most teenagers wouldn't have done what me and Precious did, so I think we did real good. I remember I was in the hospital with my sickle cell and I was telling a nurse about us, and she said, "I'm real proud of you because most peo-

Lloyd's Kitchen

ple wouldn't have done what you did. Things probably aren't going too good for you-all now, but God is looking after you and he likes what you've done. Your day will come sometime, and you all will be blessed." I like to think about that.

What are your feelings about the future?
I want to go back to school. I want to get a good job. But my main thing is to move away from these projects. I don't care what it takes. I don't know how I'm going to do it, but I'm getting away from here! I hate it—this neighborhood, the people shooting each other, killing each other. I'm going to be twenty-three next month and I just want to do something with my life before it's over.

Thank you.

•   •   •

I talked to my five-year-old nephew, Mookie—my sister Precious's son—in my room.

Lloyd: Mookie, what do you want to be when you grow up?
Mookie: Superman.
Lloyd: You can't be Superman.
Mookie: Then I'm gonna get a job.
Lloyd: What do you have to do first? First you got to go to . . .
Mookie: Uhhh . . . School!
Lloyd: Then you got to go to . . .
Mookie: Uhhh . . .
Lloyd: College.
Mookie: Ain't nobody in college!
Lloyd: Yeah, there's a whole bunch of people in college.
Mookie: What happens when they get out of college?
Lloyd: They get a job.
Mookie: Where they stay?
Lloyd: They can live anywhere they want to. They can buy big houses, cars—anything they want.
Mookie: You got to be big to go to college?
Lloyd: Yup. Got to be my size or a little shorter. If you are not my size or a little shorter and you're in college, something's wrong. Mookie, do you know what it means not to be able to get out of something?

191

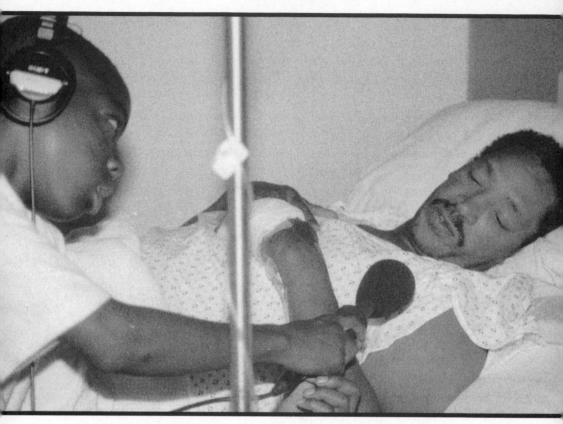

Lloyd and Chill

Mookie: You'll be stuck?

Lloyd: Yeah, you'll be stuck in it. That's how the projects are.

Mookie: What's the projects?

Lloyd: These are the projects. That's where black people live who get aid checks. You're living in the projects. It ain't easy.

Mookie: What ain't easy?

Lloyd: Trying to get out of the projects. It's hard to get out of them. You got to be a hundred percent confident to make it out.

Mookie: What's that?

Lloyd: Confident? To have faith in yourself. Now it's 1996. We got four more years to go till the year 2000. . . .

Mookie: We learn how to count in school—1996, one, two, three, four, five . . .

Lloyd: You smart, man.

Mookie: What you mean?

Lloyd: You don't know what smart is?

Mookie: I got a smart mouth?

Lloyd: No, you're smart. You know a lot of stuff. . . . Hey, Mookie?

Mookie: What?

Lloyd: You know what?

Mookie: What?

Lloyd: No matter what happens, I won't let you turn out to be wild. You're gonna go to school, get an education, and get out of here. You got to believe in yourself. You're gonna make it.

•   •   •

My father, Chill, is still not doing too good. I spent a couple of days looking for him around The Wells to do an interview, but I couldn't find him anywhere. Finally I called my grandmother, and she told me that he was at Doctors Hospital in Hyde Park.

Why are you here?

Chill: Well, by my drinking so much, I have seizures. I used to drink two and three pints of wine every day, and the alcohol ate my brain cells. So last week I was cooking, heating up a pot with grease in it, and all of a sudden I had a seizure and fell on the floor. I tried to grab the pot with my hand and I burned it real bad. Lucky I woke up out of my seizure or the house would have caught on fire and I would have been dead.

How has your life changed since 1993?
It hasn't changed. Not really. I'm not able to work now because of my liver—I only have about thirty percent of my liver left from drinking. I used to get drunk every day, but I have slowed down. I had been clean in an alcoholic program for two months—I got a diploma for that—but I relapsed when I got out again. Really, my life has been up and down. I'm up one day and down the next day. That's all I can say.

How have I changed?
Well, Lloyd, you have changed a lot. You are getting very intelligent and learning real well. But what I want you to do is to go to school every day. I'm worried about your grades. I'm worried about you in the streets. I know you gamble a lot. You used to watch me shoot pool and think you could do it. You always used to say, "There's a pool table in there, Daddy!" 'Cause you loved to watch me beat people. But I don't like gambling anymore—I've seen people get killed over that. I know about that part of life, and I don't ever want you to be like that—because it's a dirty, rotten, low-down life. Quit listening to people on the streets and grow up to be a man. That's all I want out of you.

Why are you still drinking?
I have a lot on my mind—mostly about my children and what's happening on the streets. I go out and I see killings, and I think about my kids and start drinking. It's like I'm running away from my thoughts.

Do you still think about my mother?
Oh yes. I dream about her because I love her a lot. When she died is when I started really going on the drinking spells. We had been together seventeen years. She was young and pretty and she had a good mind. But she died from drinking, just like I am dying from it.

When you die, do you want to be buried next to Mom?
Yes, I would like to be buried next to Lynn. If I don't stop drinking, I may not have more than six months to live, 'cause my liver is down to about thirty percent. I have been trying awful hard to clean myself up. Trying the best I can. That's all I can do—give it my best and maybe one day it'll turn around. Just hoping that one day I'll wake up and it'll just turn around.

CHAPTER 24

PARTING WORDS

LeAlan: What's up? It's LeAlan and Lloyd coming at you one last time, going to say good-bye and give you our parting words. We're seventeen now, almost eighteen. We were only what in '93—thirteen?

Lloyd: We came a long way!

LeAlan: A long way. We've done three major things in our life now: this book and our two documentaries. What do you think about this?

Lloyd: It's one of the best things that ever happened to me. Without this I don't know what I'd be doing. It helped me out a lot.

LeAlan: What are some of the things that we did that stay in your mind?

Lloyd: Everything. Everything.

LeAlan: Like what?

Lloyd: Walking around, interviewing people, going to the lake, riding buses, going out of town to win awards. Everything.

LeAlan: I guess we found an oasis. Our little oasis in the ghetto.

Lloyd: Now I just can't wait to get out of here.

LeAlan: I'll be gone in August. What's that—seven months? It seems like eternity, but I've almost made it. . . .

Lloyd: You ain't made it until you're out of here. The other day they were shooting right outside my house and I thought I was fixing to get shot. I didn't know where to run, so I just ran into somebody's hallway and closed the door. I was spooked.

LeAlan (left) and Lloyd

LeAlan: I bet you woke up and went to school the next morning, though, didn't you?

Lloyd: Heck yeah!

LeAlan: People forget about stuff like that. Man, I think if we make it out of here we deserve a Medal of Honor or a Purple Heart. Because if you aren't wounded physically, you're wounded spiritually. We deserve a Purple Heart coming out of this motherfucker. I believe we've been in a damn war.

Lloyd: It has been a war. . . .

LeAlan: And now we're grown almost. No more kiddy games, no more wishing on a star. Things have changed. And things have changed with me and you.

Lloyd: I guess we're not as close as we used to be.

LeAlan: You still got a little more child in you, and I've grown up a little more. Like the jokes we told then are just not as funny now. . . .

Lloyd: We're still friends, but we just don't kick it like we used to—like going on bus rides—because we got older. We had to separate—we couldn't be together all our life.

LeAlan: But you're still my best friend. . . .

Lloyd: That hasn't changed.

LeAlan: It's just that as you get older . . . over time . . . things change. . . .

Lloyd: We grew up.

LeAlan: And you went through a few problems, but that ain't going to stop you.

Lloyd: I know.

LeAlan: But you should be graduating with us, man.

Lloyd: I know—I just start crying sometimes thinking about that. But I'm going to make it.

LeAlan: Got to make it, man. Got to.

Lloyd: I just can't see myself staying here. I can't see it.

LeAlan: We got to make it.

Lloyd: I just can't fall. I went up too high. All these things that we've accomplished—I just can't fall down.

LeAlan: But with God on our side, we're going to make it.

Lloyd: It's hard, though. It ain't easy.

LeAlan: It ain't easy, but we're going to make it. I'll be out of this place in a heartbeat—literally a heartbeat.

197

Lloyd: What college are you going to?

LeAlan: Howard. I hope Howard. So next year you're going to be here by yourself, man.

Lloyd: But I'm coming right up out of it too, right behind you. Might take another year, but I'm getting out of here. I just think about that every night.

LeAlan: So if you go next year, what's going to happen to Mookie and Rere?

Lloyd: I'm going to move us all up out of here!

LeAlan: Me too. I'm gonna get my grandmother a home. When I do that, I'll be happy to the day I die!

Lloyd: Yup.

LeAlan: So now it's over. We go our separate ways. It's kind of sad, but I guess some way or another we both made it. I believe we wouldn't have let each other fail. We got to sign off now, so is there anything else you would like to say about the end of our partnership?

Lloyd: I wish it wasn't the end. That's all.

LeAlan: Peace.

Lloyd: Peace.

CHAPTER 25

OUR AMERICA

Hello. This is LeAlan Jones with the last chapter. It's November 19, 1996, and I want to leave you with some final words about our America.

We live in two different Americas. In the ghetto, our laws are totally different, our language is totally different, and our lives are totally different. I've never felt American, I've only felt African-American. An American is supposed to have life, liberty, prosperity, and happiness. But an African-American is due pain, poverty, stress, and anxiety. As an African-American I have experienced beautiful things, but the majority of the things I've experienced are not beautiful. And I don't even have it as bad as most—there are millions of young men and women living the struggle even harder than me. As children, they have to make day-to-day decisions about whether to go to school or whether to go on the corner and sell drugs. As children, they know that there may not be a tomorrow. Why are African-American children faced with this dilemma at such an early age? Why must they look down the road to a future that they might never see? What have my people done to this country to deserve this?

And yet I am supposed to feel American. I am supposed to be patriotic. I am supposed to love this system that has been detrimental to the lives of my people. It's hard for me to say how I'm an American when I live in a second America—an America that doesn't wave the red, white, and blue flag with fifty stars for fifty states. I live in a community that waves a white flag because we have almost given up. I live in a community where on the walls are the names of fallen comrades of war. I live in a second America. I live here not because I chose to, but because I have to. I hate to sound militant, but this is the way I feel.

I wonder sometimes, "Why am I alive? What is my purpose?" And I can always find a reason. But for a kid whose mother is a crack addict and who doesn't have a father and doesn't have a meal at night and has holes in his shoes when he walks the streets and can barely read and can barely communicate his feelings (which is almost the usual characteristics of a child from the ghetto), when he asks himself the question "What is my reason for being? What is my purpose?" what can he tell himself? These are the thoughts that go on in my mind and really mesmerize me.

Some people might look at me and say, "He's just some little nigger from the ghetto that knows some big words." Well, true. That might be. But listen to what I'm saying. I know you don't want to hear about the pain and suffering that goes on in "that" part of the city. I know you don't want to hear about the kids getting shot in "that" part of the city. But little do you know that "that" part of the city is your part of the city too. This is our neighborhood, this is our city, and this is our America. And we must somehow find a way to help one another. We must come together—no matter what you believe in, no matter how you look—and find some concrete solutions to the problems of the ghetto. Right now we are at the point of no return. We've got to make a change, because if we don't we'll go into the millennium in total disarray. But I believe it's going to be all right. Somehow, some way, I believe in my heart that we can make this happen. Not me by myself. Not you by yourself. I'm talking about all of us as one, living together in our America.

This is LeAlan Jones on November 19, 1996. I hope I survive. I hope I survive. I hope I survive. Signing off. Peace.

LeAlan Jones attends Florida State University, where he is majoring in criminology. LeAlan is the National Junior Spokesperson for the No Dope Express and has lectured across the country. His honors for the radio documentaries *Ghetto Life 101* and *Remorse* include the Livingston Award, the George Foster Peabody, and the grand prize from the Robert F. Kennedy Journalism Awards—the first time a radio program has ever received that honor.

Lloyd Newman attends Future Commons High School in Chicago. He enjoys poetry, chess, rap music, and driving. Lloyd shares in each of the above journalism awards for his work as reporter and coproducer of the radio programs.

John Brooks was born and raised in Cabrini Green. At the age of twelve, he enrolled in an after-school photography class and won a district competition. He has been taking pictures ever since. John is married and has two children.

David Isay is the author of *Holding On,* and a regular contributor to NPR's *All Things Considered.* Over the past ten years, he has received every major award in broadcasting as well as a Guggenheim Fellowship. David is president of Sound Portraits Productions, a not-for-profit radio production company in New York City.

If you would like to order CD or cassette copies of the two public radio documentaries on which *Our America* is based: *Ghetto Life 101* (1993) and *Remorse: The 14 Stories of Eric Morse* (1996), please call (212) 353-3880, or visit Sound Portraits Productions on the World Wide Web: http://www.soundports.org. Proceeds go to LeAlan Jones, Lloyd Newman, and Sound Portraits Productions, a nonprofit radio production company.